A Tra
Siberian
Odyssey

5,000 miles by train from Beijing to Moscow

by

Kate Young

Part of the Trans-Siberian Writing Challenge
21 September to 10 October 2008
transsibwriter.wordpress.com

All profits from the sale of this book will go to the
Earl Mountbatten Hospice on the Isle of Wight
(*www.iwhospice.org*)

A Proudhorse (IOW) Book
E-mail: *proudhorseiow@googlemail.com*

Enjoy the tale!
Kate Young

My thanks to:

My friend Nikki Bennett-Willetts, my fiancé Hugh Couch and to my family for being so supportive and to Steve Collins for helping me with the finer points of design.

Published by:

Proudhorse Enterprises (IOW),

Newport, Isle of Wight.

proudhorseiow@googlemail.com

Printed by:

Printondemand-worldwide.com,
9 Culley Court,
Orton Southgate,
Peterborough,
PE2 6WA.

ISBN: 978-184426-625-8

About the charity

Established in 1982, the Earl Mountbatten Hospice is a registered charity (No. 1039086) and since April 2006, it has been responsible for the palliative care of terminally-ill adults on the Isle of Wight.

This flagship hospice caters for around 800 patients a year with a wide range of life-shortening conditions, including cancer, brain tumours, motor neurone disease, congestive heart failure and kidney failure.

It costs £3.7 million a year to keep the hospice open at the time of writing (early 2009) and although the charity receives a grant from the Isle of Wight Primary Care Trust for around a third of this sum, it still has to raise around £2.2 million on its own every year.

Put more simply, it requires £7,000 a day to keep the hospice doors open and charity has to raise £4,500 of this amount. That is £4,500 to find each day, every day.

One of its major fundraising events is the annual Walk The Wight, in which people from across the UK and further afield walk across the island from east to west. In 2008, the walk raised more than £350,000 for the hospice – which paid for approximately one-tenth of its annual costs. The hospice also runs its own lottery to help generate funds.

The hospice has well under 20 beds, but provides excellent day-care facilities, as well as its innovative Hospice@Home service. The latter gives people who would prefer to die at home surrounded by their family the peace of mind that they will be properly cared for at all times.

There are lots of ways in which people can help the Earl Mountbatten Hospice raise the vital cash it needs to keep going. Find out more on the hospice website at *www.iwhospice.org*

A Trans-Siberian Odyssey

A beginning

THERE can be few things sadder than the death of a young person and the apparent death of an ambition. But both have inspired my Trans-Siberian Writing Challenge and the resulting travel diary.

The young person was my colleague Jeremy Price, who died at the Earl Mountbatten Hospice on the Isle of Wight in October 2007 aged 34 – just two years older than I was at the time.

I had worked on and off with Jeremy at the Isle of Wight County Press newspaper for about eight years and like many journalists, he left the newspaper to work for another publication on the mainland and later returned to us. But throughout all this time he was fighting a serious battle with a brain tumour.

When Jeremy returned to the newspaper for his second stint, he sat next to me. I was planning this long trip to China and the Trans-Siberian Railway with a group of women writers from across the UK. We were going to write a book together whilst doing this iconic journey.

Jeremy piped up one day: "What you need is a challenge to keep you all writing!" We laughed. We kept coming up with daft ideas about how we could keep writing – longest silly poem, comic verses, loony limericks – who knows, maybe there was a Roger McGough amongst us (Jeremy's favourite poet).

It wasn't until after Jeremy's death and following the group of women writers dwindling from the original 11 to just two, that I felt I should still do some sort of a challenge and raise money for the Earl Mountbatten Hospice, which had looked after Jeremy so well in his final days.

My travelling companion, Nikki Bennett-Willetts, is a Bath-based poet and I am a journalist, so a book created between us could have been a rather bizarre mixture of styles. Instead, we decided to work on our own individual writing projects whilst travelling together.

I found myself challenged to write at least 100 A5 pages during the 18-day trip – so as well as travelling more than 5,000 miles overland and seeing the highlights of China, Mongolia, Siberia and Russia, I would have to write at least six pages a day to reach my target.

In my day-to-day work as a journalist, I write about commercial subjects such as motoring, bridal, home improvements, fashion and beauty, places to visit on the Isle of Wight, Christmas shopping, new businesses opening and much more. It is a job I have done for ten years and done it very well, but I find myself getting increasingly bored as predictably the same things come up again and again every single year.

As a child, my ambitions were to travel and write books. A lack of funds meant I didn't venture abroad until I was 27, but during the past six years I have managed to get away to destinations in Europe, North Africa and Asia and have recently ventured as far afield as Croatia, Morocco, Tunisia and Turkey.

Regarding writing, my degree is in Creative Writing and Publishing with Political Studies and I have written numerous prize-winning poems and short stories, so there is a writer in there somewhere!

By setting a writing challenge to write an unforgettable travel diary whilst on the once-in-a-lifetime trip, I hope to rekindle a lost ambition and unleash the creative beast that lies within me.

Not that you would have known it in the final 24 hours leading up to embarking on what had become known simply as the Big Trip. Indeed, the only creative thing was probably the use of my bad language!

Due to an extraordinarily busy time at work and the fact that I had been staying in someone else's house looking after their animals, I wasn't able to pack until the evening before the trip. Various people in mobile phone shops had already assured me my phone would work in Russia, Mongolia and China, so I rang Orange just to check I was activated for international roaming in all three countries.

The guy in the call centre proceeded to laugh. Apparently, Pay As You Go customers like me were fine in Russia, but the phone wouldn't work in Mongolia or China. The only solution was to go contract – minimum of 12 months.

"So put me on contract now – I fly out tomorrow!" I howled down the phone. The reply was he couldn't, because it required a different sym card that had to be send by post. Blast!

The same evening – less than 24 hours before my flight – my digital camera developed problems, so my fiancé Hugh loaned me his, which meant I had a new camera to get used to as well as a new contract phone (yes, I went to the nearest phone shop on Sunday morning before I left the Island).

On the coach heading for Heathrow, I found myself thinking about Jeremy and how he would have felt about me taking off on this mad writing challenge – I know he would have laughed about my technological dunderheadedness.

Jeremy was a real family man and he adored his wife and young son, but he was also always an extraordinary reporter. When he was working for the Colchester Gazette newspaper in Essex, he wrote about his 'daily zapping' and his illness in a weekly column. In 2004, it was entered into the Norwich Union-supported Medical Journalism Awards and was commended in the feature category. Jeremy was the only regional newspaper writer to reach the final that year.

In 2006/7, when he had returned to the Isle of Wight County Press the difference in him was marked in that his short-term memory wasn't terribly good. But he was a very precise note-taker and always coped with his illness with such good humour.

I hope I have been able to record my incredible trip with the same level of precision and good humour that Jeremy always showed.

On our way

I WAS on my way. Hugh gave me a lift to the ferry and I caught the coach to Heathrow, where I met up with Nikki. Both of us were practically electric with excitement.

We had only met twice before and there is a considerable difference between us – Nikki is in her 50s and divorced with a grown-up son, while I am 33 and wondering if the Big Trip is a last hurrah before I settle down with Hugh. There is only so long a woman should hold off having children after all – biological clock and all that.

There is a certain level of trepidation too, as Nikki and I are practically strangers embarking on a long trip where we are going to be sharing accommodation and experiences throughout. But we are fairly confident that we will get on well and after I have typed a new post on the Big Trip charity fundraising blog, we toast the forthcoming adventure with a large glass of wine, before boarding the plane to Hong Kong.

In the build-up to the Big Trip, people kept asking me why we had chosen to do the Trans-Siberian Railway, starting in the Chinese capital just a few days after the end of the Beijing Olympics and Paralympics of 2008.

Apart from the fact the Trans-Siberian Railway is a truly

11

iconic journey that has been done by numerous famous travel writers, artists and other people, it also goes through some of the world's least visited countryside and has a fascinating history.

Indeed, the celebrated travel writer Eric Newby famously wrote in The Big Red Train Ride that the Trans-Siberian is the big train ride and all the rest are peanuts compared to it.

The Trans-Siberian Railway is not one route, but a collection of five different ones. The most famous is also the longest, which travels from Vladivostock on the Sea of Japan to Moscow and is known as the Trans-Siberian. A further spur of this line continues from Moscow to St Petersburg, which is often nicknamed the Venice of the North.

The Trans-Siberian line is 9,288km in length between Vladivostock and Moscow and is generally recognised as the longest direct railway line in the world. It covers ten time zones in total and is longer than both the Great Wall of China and the US Route 66.

The next longest route is the Trans-Manchurian, which is 9,001km and goes from Beijing to Moscow via Harbin, which means it bypasses Mongolia. It takes a day longer to go via Harbin to Beijing than to cross Mongolia, but the Trans-Manchurian is very popular in January because of Harbin's legendary ice festival, when the town is filled with sculptures.

Our choice was the third major route, the Trans-Mongolian line, which goes from Beijing via the Mongolian capital of Ulaanbaatar to Ulan Ude and on to Moscow. This is a mere 7,865km (almost 5,000 miles).

The Trans-Siberian also includes two smaller routes, the Baikal-Amur Mainline (BAM), which skirts the northern edge of the mighty Lake Baikal in Siberia and AYaM, which starts near Bamovskaya in the Russian Far East.

Incredibly, only 19 per cent of the Trans-Siberian is in Europe – the remainder east of the Ural Mountains is in Asia and a small obelisk marks the Europe/Asia line at 1,778km. There is always a bit of fuss on the train as people try to spot it as they go by.

Few people know that the ballet legend Rudolf Nureyev was born on the Trans-Siberian Railway near Irkutsk in Siberia, while his mother, Farida, was travelling to Vladivostock because his father, Hamat, was a Red Army political commissar and was stationed there.

The actual history of the railway is fascinating too. While many visitors today consider it to be a sort of slow boat to China, the Trans-Siberian Railway was actually founded as a result of great rivalry between Russian and English merchants.

The Russians' plan was simple – to outmanoeuvre the English merchants in China and India by offering an express route that would rush even perishable goods from Asia to Europe in just over a week, which would help cater for the developing tastes in Europe for silks, spices, tropical fruits and other exotica.

Tsar Alexander III gave the project his official sanction in 1886 with the words: "It is time, high time!" and on May 31, 1891, his son the Tsarevich Nicholas laid the foundation stone at Vladivostock.

Ironically the Tsarevich - who became the last Tsar, Nicholas II – would take his final journey on the railway under communist rule, when he was placed under house arrest as a prisoner on board the Trans-Siberian on his way to his death.

The main route to Vladivostock was built between 1891 and 1916 – indeed the industrious Russians ensured all but the Lake Baikal section was completed within the first ten years and the railway became extremely popular for transportation of goods and passengers alike.

After the Russian Revolution in 1917, it became increasingly difficult for foreigners to obtain permits for Siberia and not until the 1960s did Westerners begin to use the railway again.

In the early 1980s restrictions for travelling in China were eased and the railway provided interesting routes to China and Mongolia, while the demise of communist Russia in the 1990s opened up the whole of Siberia to foreign travellers.

Today, around 30 per cent of Russian exports travel on the line and the train carries about 20,000 containers a year to Europe, as well of hordes of locals and travellers.

As a child, when things went missing in our house, the standard joke was: "Oh, it will probably turn up in Outer Mongolia!" Part of wanting to do the Trans-Sib stems from itching to find out what that mythical place of my childhood mind really looks like.

Visiting Russia is more affordable than ever before and with the Olympics in Beijing and a chance to see Genghis Khan's ancient land of Mongolia, I felt the autumn of 2008 was the time to seize the bit between my teeth and finally do the journey of a lifetime.

Back to our journey and Nikki and I have just boarded the biggest plane I have ever seen in all my life – a 747. I guess it's a shock to me because I have only ever flown short-haul before with a maximum four hours in the sky. Nikki says she has been on one plenty of times – but she did live in the USA for some time and had to fly trans-Atlantic.

Unfortunately we are about an hour late taking off because someone checked a suitcase into the hold, but didn't turn up for the flight, so everything had to come off so the offending bag could be removed.

So it is after 10pm when we take off and I thought we would get into the air and go to sleep, but no – a full meal was served and I made the mistake of having more wine with it, not realising how much it might affect me later.

I was shattered after hurtling around all morning trying to solve my phone problems, so I went straight to sleep. I woke up feeling hot in the middle of the night, went to get a drink of water and whop – I fainted. I was only out momentarily, but I fell flat on my face, skinned my nose and now feel like a complete idiot!

Monday, September 22, 2008.

WHEN we originally got our flight booking through, what struck me was that we were taking off in London at 9.15pm and arriving at around the same time in Beijing the following night. Of course it's not really 24 hours in the sky, but lots of time zones that foul up the maths.

It is really approximately 12 hours from Heathrow to Hong Kong, then another three-and-a- half hours from Hong Kong to Beijing.

Not that we took off on time anyway, following last night's security alert. Although our British Airways flight has been going along at a good speed, we haven't made that time up, which means Nikki and I will have to make a mad dash through Hong Kong airport to catch our connecting flight later.

I can't praise the airline staff enough for being so

thoroughly nice to me last night, despite the fact it was my own fault. I feel a right twit this morning (and I look it too!).

Despite everything, I have slept well, had super meals, made the in-flight entertainment work (a rarity) and even watched the recently-released Jackie Chan film The Forbidden Kingdom to get me into the China mood. Twelve hours on the first leg of a flight is just about as long haul as it gets and it has been really turbulent in places, but it's a first long-haul route that I will never forget!

As I write this, we are on approach to land at Hong Kong airport where we have been warned it is 35 deg C and humid, which sounds pretty uncomfortable to me. But we are now at least an hour late, which means our connecting flight will leave in about 50 minutes time, so after we have landed, it will be pretty much off one plane and straight onto the next one!

Fortunately, William Li from BA is waiting for us as we step off of the plane and he ushered us through the transfer desks and security to the right gate just before boarding started. Incredibly he had studied in Manchester, as had Nikki's son.

Our flight turned out to be a Dragonair incorporating the Cathay Pacific and Air China flights and just before boarding I switched on both my mobile phones and get this – they both worked! Both picked up a network and I believe I can send messages off of both – so much for my old phone being dual-band and wouldn't work!

Alas, Hong Kong remained wrapped in mist for the duration that we were there, so we couldn't really see the beautiful harbour, either when we came in or when we left again.

But once our Hong Kong-Beijing flight got above the clouds, we were treated to a beautiful sunset and no sooner were we into the flight proper than there was another meal served up, so that's dinner, breakfast and lunch in our '24-hour' flight.

After the meal, I browsed through a copy of the South China Morning Post, an English broadsheet newspaper and filled in my arrivals card ready for customs when we reach Beijing.

Then Nikki and I settled down to our writing and I found myself thinking of the other ladies who were originally interested in coming on this trip – I hope they know what they are missing!

Another curious thing about this trip is that today Nikki and I have flown in 16 or so hours what it will take us three weeks to return across overland. That's another unique thing about the trip – it really brings home the sheer time difference between various forms of travel.

Many people would argue that we were rushing the Trans-Sib by doing it in three weeks. Indeed you can take months exploring the railway and stopping off at the 80-odd different towns and villages along the Moscow-Vladivostock leg. Add the other routes and I suspect you could happily spend years on it.

Furthermore, the Trans-Sib actually links up with lots of other train routes, so you can just keep travelling. For example, we looked into travelling via rail back from Moscow to London via Berlin and Brussels, but abandoned the idea of this two-day route because we felt we would not be able to keep the whole trip within a three-week time limit.

European networks are excellent and you can go for miles, but for a more unusual trip, you could travel around China by train from Beijing, follow direct rail links into Vietnam, follow the Turkestan-Siberia (Turksib) railway along the Silk Road back to Europe or take a ferry from Vladivostock to Japan.

In recent years, Russia has actively negotiated and financed the rebuilding of the railway between North and South Korea and the Vladivostock to Pyongang line is apparently now open, though I am not certain how easy it is to get a ticket for it!

In planning the Big Trip, I knew we would be in for some very changeable weather conditions and having been told it was hot and raining in Beijing when I checked the BBC Weather online five-day forecast back in the UK, the pilot is telling us a different story – it's a nice 24 deg C and dry, which is good news because it will hopefully mean we will have fabulous views of the Great Wall of China when we visit tomorrow.

We are later than expected on arrival in Beijing and the first thing I notice is that all the colourful Olympic flags are still up in the terminal and literally every surface is clean and shiny. It is an amazing terminal and it is hard to believe that only a few days ago it would have been full of Paralympics competitors – or Olympians just a week or two before. Imagine the famous feet that have trod before us on their way to sporting glory.

Unfortunately, the train to baggage reclaim is broken, so there is a big queue for the shuttle bus and we caught the third or fourth one. But when we got to baggage reclaim there were no suitcases waiting for us – clearly our luggage was lost somewhere between Heathrow Terminal 5 and Beijing.

We saw the girl at the Air China desk, who checked on

her computer and said our cases had made it to Hong Kong and were on the next plane, so they should be here within an hour. So we drifted around in the airport and drank water from folding paper cups that reminded me of white pay-packet envelopes and sure enough, our cases arrived on the next flight.

We grabbed a taxi with a Chinese driver, who read the address I gave him and took us into the city to the Red Wall Hotel and after a bit of confusion about the fare, which was soon sorted out, we checked in at about midnight. On reaching our room, I said hello to the Olympic city, then we unpacked a little before bed.

Hello Beijing

WE have discovered why it is called the Red Wall Hotel – there is a whopping red-bricked building outside my window, so no view then! Pity, as we are within a stone's throw of the Forbidden City.

We got up early and went down to breakfast to discover a full-blown buffet with loads of Chinese specialities including won ton soup, which I just had to have.

We met with Sally, our enthusiastic Dragon Tours guide, who explained that she had an (unpronounceable) Chinese name which meant 'pretty flowing river', but English speakers called her Sally.

Our party numbered eight from different hotels across the city and as well as us, there was an older couple from Singapore, a younger couple from France and two girls from Russia, so a thoroughly international minibus-load.

Beijing is a city packed with bicycles and hordes spun by us and we forged our way through the morning traffic. Sally pointed out the Olympic velodrome and the statue of a famous farmer on a horse who had seized power at the end of the Ming Dynasty in 1644 and had ruled for just 42 days.

The Ming Tombs was our first port of call. A total of 13 of the 16 Ming Dynasty (1368-1644) emperors are buried at the tombs, which are situated at the bottom of Heavenly Longevity Mountain and guarded by Dragon Mountain and Tiger Mountain. This site is some 55km from the centre of Beijing and is actually very large, though we saw only a small part of it.

We went to Chang Ling, which is one of only a handful of tombs open to the public, but it really was an incredible sight. One of the first things that struck me about these wonderful historical Chinese buildings is that they are made almost entirely of wood, yet they have survived for hundreds of years.

Chang Ling was packed with tour groups, with many of the leaders carrying little flags like Sally's – yet almost all the visitors were Chinese, even though it was a working day in the city.

As we stepped into the massive building, I was amazed at the hugely-ornate painted ceiling and by the huge amount of Yuan (Chinese currency) people had left at the foot of the large Buddha dominating the room – which turned out to be a museum.

Sally started to show us round the crowded museum and it was hard to see the display cases over the heads of so many others, but there were gold bowls and ingots, jade jewellery, Ming vases, beautiful clothes and head-dresses belonging to the emperors and empresses and all the things they were buried with. It was extraordinary to think of all these riches being put into the ground with them and reminiscent of the rulers of ancient Egypt whose pyramids were built centuries earlier.

It was also tragic to hear of the poor concubines, who had to be sacrificed in the event of the emperor's death. Some emperors had up to 3,000 concubines, all aged between 14 and 18.

Chang Ling is the tomb of Emperor Yongle (pronounced Yong Lee), who was the third emperor of the Ming Dynasty and died in 1428. He was felt to be a very good ruler and was responsible for much development in Beijing, including building the Forbidden City and the Temple Of Heaven. It was Yongle who chose the site of the tombs and he was the first to be buried there. Hence his tomb is the largest and most centrally located – and it has never been excavated.

Stepping out of the museum, you discover a courtyard with a massive yellow incense burner on one side and the most extraordinary gate in the middle.

Sally explained that we would go round the Gate Between Two Walls on our way to the next building, instead of through it, because the gate represented the step between the living and the dead.

The imposing building which loomed up in front of us was the Soul Tower, the gateway to the underworld. Although heaving with tour groups, its thick walls and cool interior gave it a really spiritual feeling and from the top of the tower, I could see other tomb buildings punctuating the green swathes reaching out to the mountains.

On returning to ground level, we approached the Gate Between Two Walls. Tradition has it that women are required to step through with their right leg first and men with their left to represent Yin and Yang and when you step though, you recite the Chinese words for 'I am back already' to ensure that your soul remains intact – which our group and many others did en-mass.

After the Ming Tombs, we took a short drive to a government-run jade carving factory and Sally explained that the Chinese believe jade is good for the heart and represents good fortune, so almost everyone wears jade jewellery or owns a carving. She also told us that different animals have different meanings – a running horse means success will come soon while a fish is a symbol of great wealth.

A young man showed us round the factory and explained that jade comes in all colours, told us how it is carved and showed us how to tell the real from the fake. We also saw a suit of armour made of jade and an exquisitely-carved fish pond, complete with live goldfish swimming around in it!

It is said that jade glows with the vitality of the owner and if the owner becomes ill, the jade becomes tarnished – which may explain the origins of our word 'jaded.'

We had lunch at the factory and then we continued to the Great Wall of China at Badaling. No matter how much you have read about it, or seen it on television, the Great Wall is an arresting sight in the flesh.

In his book Riding The Iron Rooster, travel writer Paul Theroux likens the Great Wall to a dragon, which is regarded as both a good omen and a guardian symbol in China. He said he found a bewitching similarity between the Chinese dragon and the Great Wall of China and describes its crenellations as like fins on a dragon's back and its bricks like scales. He said it looked serpentine and protective, wrapping itself round endlessly from one end of the world to the other.

I don't know if the Great Wall can be seen in space or not, but it is truly impressive – it winds its way thousands of miles from Shanhaiguan in the Yellow Sea right up to the Gobi Desert.

The first parts were built in the 5th Century BC, but the present wall was largely planned in around 220BC by Qin Shi Huangdi, the first Chinese emperor and founder of the empire. It was designed to keep invaders out, though it didn't always succeed, as proved by the marauding Mongols in the 13th Century.

Badaling is probably the most heavily renovated and popular section, largely due to the fact it is only around 80km from Beijing, so it is a popular day-trip destination.

The Great Wall was originally designed so that five or six horsemen could ride side by side along it and fortified towers and garrisons completed the defences. Today, it is hard to see how you could ride horses along it, because there are some very steep sections and lots of large, uneven-sized steps with slippery patches – health and safety, eat your heart out!

Badaling is quite touristy, right down to having bears to feed in a compound near the coach park, but you do get a real sense of how important the wall is to the Chinese and I think at least 95 per cent of today's visitors were Chinese.

Chairman Mao climbed to the Eighth Watchtower in the North at Badaling when well into his seventies and he proclaimed that anyone who could reach this point was a hero, so I just had to do it!

To save time, Sally suggested taking the sliding cars part-way up the hill to the fourth tower and this was great fun – they were just like bumper cars right down to the brightly-coloured plastic, except they were fixed onto a ground rail which pulled them up the hill. When we came back down on these, the young man driving a long chain of them let the brake off and we flew down the slope.

After climbing the Great Wall, Sally took us to a Chinese medicine centre, where we got to have our feet soaked in hot tea, then massaged. A Chinese doctor looked at us all too and told me some very interesting things about how taking ginseng could improve my energy levels.

When we finally got back to our hotel, we popped out in search of a restaurant and discovered scenes from a movie being filmed right outside. We went in anyway and when our food came, it was far more than we had expected and it was beautifully presented. I persuaded one of the staff to show me how to use chopsticks in the Chinese way and dug in.

I have been following Ching-He Huang of the BBC2 series Chinese Food Made Easy, who said that one of the important aspects of Chinese food is the philosophy of yin and yang – all ingredients have one of these elements attached to them and yin foods are cooling while yang foods are heat-giving. Traditionally Chinese cooks would try to balance them in any one dish. Cooking techniques also impart a yin or yang element to a dish – stir-frying and steaming are yin, while deep-frying is yang.

After finishing our monster meal – which was both tasty and affordable – we went back to the hotel and I put an entry on my blog before going back to our room to read about Chinese mythology.

According to Chinese mythology, Zhongguo (the middle kingdom), the world and the universe all owe their existence to a giant named Pan Gu, who once lived in an enormous egg. He sliced the egg in half to create Heaven and Earth, then stood like Atlas between the two halves, holding them apart.

After countless millennia, Pan Gu died. His left eye became the sun and his right eye the moon, while his body turned into mountain ranges and his blood into flowing rivers. His perspiration became rain, his hair became vegetation and his bones were transformed into minerals and rocks.

Somewhat unflatteringly, the myth goes on to tell us that the human race arose from the lice on Pan Gu's body!

WE woke up late this morning – so conversely our tour guide, whose English name was Jessica, was early.

We were the first ones on the minibus, but it transpired that we were a smaller group today, just Nikki and I and two German gentlemen.

I have been thinking about the numerous things we owe to the Chinese. China is the motherland of several inventions. Imagine Bonfire Night without fireworks, or navigation without a compass or windy days without kites to fly. These familiar objects, which we take for granted in the West, owe their origins to the skill of the Chinese in centuries past.

Papermaking was unknown in Europe before the 11-12th Century AD, but can be traced back in China to the 3rd Century BC. Among the things paper was used for was the construction of kites, which were flown by normal people for recreation, by Taoist monks as a meditative exercise and even by some intrepid adventurers for experiments in manned flight!

The 4th Century BC saw the Chinese using the world's first magnetic compasses in the form of lodestones (pieces of naturally magnetic iron ore) and by about 132 AD they had developed another sensitive directional instrument: a seismograph, able to detect earth tremors hundreds of miles away. It was not until 1703 that the first working European seismograph was invented.

In England, the father of modern seismology was John Milne, who lived on the Isle of Wight. His house is still standing and he is buried in a graveyard in my home town of Newport.

Possibly the most momentous of China's discoveries was

26

gunpowder. It was first created in the 9th Century AD by alchemists seeking the elixir of life! In due course it was used for fireworks, which probably inspired the invention of military rocket-launchers. Guns and cannons followed and were enthusiastically adopted by the powers of Europe as soon as they heard about such weapons in the late 12th Century.

Astonishing as it might sound, China had been unified for nearly 1,500 years before the first eye-witness accounts of this extraordinary eastern land reached Europe. These accounts came from brothers Nicolo and Maffeo Polo, Venetian merchants who travelled across the great Tien Shan mountains and overland to China in the early 1260s.

After a nine-year round trip, they returned to Europe with fantastic tales of their adventures, most notably their welcoming reception at the court of China's first Mongol ruler, the emperor Kublai Khan, grandson of Genghis.

In 1271, the Polo brothers set out again, this time with Nicolo's 17-year-old son, Marco. Four years later they reached Kublai Khan's summer palace at Shangdu. The young Marco – now 21 – so impressed the emperor that during the next 17 years he undertook many missions on the Great Khan's behalf and travelled throughout the land as his personal ambassador.

The stories Marco Polo told on his eventual return to Europe seemed so far-fetched that he was accused of lying; yet the reality of what he saw was probably even more extraordinary. When urged on his deathbed to take back some of his incredible tales, Marco is reported to have whispered: "I did not tell half of what I saw, for I knew I would not be believed."

Marco's caution was well founded, for what he had

27

discovered was a country that was technologically advanced in the production of steel, ceramics and explosives; that used paper money and that had a sophisticated system of government over a land larger than all the squabbling nations of Europe put together.

Small wonder people were unable to believe Marco Polo – it must have been like your best friend coming back and telling you what the landscape looked like on Pluto!

This morning it is raining in Beijing and there are thousands of cyclists in brightly-coloured capes pouring down the road like a rainbow river. We pass the Bird's Nest Olympic stadium and the now-empty Olympic village on our way to the Summer Palace.

Situated on the outskirts of Beijing, the Summer Palace was built in the 1700s by Emperor Qianlong as a summer residence for members of the Ming Dynasty. It was originally known as the Palace Of Clear Rippling Water because of its location on Kunming Lake.

It didn't look too summery in the rain, but the buildings were beautiful and Jessica explained that the palace had burnt down during the Second Opium War (1856-60), but had been rebuilt in 1888 by Empress Dowager Cixi, using money that should have gone to fund the Chinese navy. In turn, she promised the navy they could train on her lake, but it wasn't big enough.

For many nations, it may be unusual to think of a woman in power at this time, but China seems to accept female rulers more easily – Empress Wu of the Tang Dynasty was the first female ruler of China and reigned from 690-705 AD.

Jessica explained that Empress Dowager Cixi was known as the Dragon Lady by the Chinese people and was not well liked. Originally a concubine, she poisoned the emperor's first wife so that she could become empress. Then when the emperor and his heir died, she put younger children on the throne so that she could keep the governing power.

She loved extravagance – she ordered more than 100 dishes to be prepared for every meal, but hardly ate any of it. She ordered fruit in the fruit bowls to be changed every six hours – she didn't eat any, but she loved its fresh fragrance. She even ordered a massive marble boat to be built on the water's edge, so she could take tea in it every day!

As well as seeing the Summer Palace with its beautiful Long Corridor and gardens, we took a boat ride on Kunming Lake, so we could see the mountains behind (bit cloudy) and were even shown a display of art painted on silk by local students – beautiful, but I didn't fancy its chances of surviving the Trans-Siberian in my case!

Next, we went to a silk factory, which was familiar territory for me, having seen similar in Turkey, but I have never watched silk duvets being made before. They use only double cocoons for duvets and hand-stretch the felt made from them. They also had silk bedlinen and clothes.

Symbolism is everywhere in China – for example, red and yellow are imperial colours, dragon is emperor, phoenix is empress and turtles, cranes and peaches are all connected with longevity.

Afterwards we went a restaurant in the grounds of the Temple Of Heaven and we were given a useful tip – if you are looking for a restaurant in China, look for lanterns outside because that means you can eat there. Handy if you cannot read the words above the door.

The Temple Of Heaven (aka Tiantan) is an extraordinary building. Recognised on the World Heritage List, this amazing structure is some 40 metres (130ft) high, is made entirely from wood and blue-glazed tiles and doesn't have a single nail in it!

Situated in the middle of a massive park, it is a superb example of Chinese Confucian architecture, dating from the Ming Dynasty. The roof tiles are deep blue to symbolise the vault of heaven and the roof is held up by 28 pillars – the four largest central ones represent the four seasons, then there is a double ring of 12, which represent the 12 months and the 12 traditional sections within a Chinese day (each is two hours long).

Like many Chinese wooden buildings, the Temple Of Heaven has been destroyed by fire several times and was last rebuilt in 1890.

Having spent some time looking at the Temple Of Heaven in awe, we were taken to a popular tea-house in the grounds to learn more about the art of tea-drinking. And in China it really is an art...

I already knew tea-drinking originated in China, hence our saying: 'Not for all the tea in China.' The Chinese were brewing it for many centuries before us, yet for many people, tea-drinking remains a quintessentially British habit. No-one knows exactly when tea – or cha, as the Chinese call it – was first brewed into a cuppa, but it was well-documented in the literature of the 4th Century and by the Tang Dynasty (618-907 AD), tea was the favourite beverage of cultivated people.

Chinese Buddhist monks lent tea a further dignity by giving it their approval and developing suitable rituals for brewing and serving it. But tea-drinking became progressively less ceremonial in China as ordinary people discovered its pleasures, particularly in pub-like tea-houses.

Once sat comfortably in our tea-house, we learned the Chinese traditionally have two types of small cup for tea – a tall thin one called the smelling cup and a bowl-shaped one for drinking only.

Next, the staff brewed us several types of tea to try, including jasmine tea, which is particularly popular in Beijing; oolong and ginseng tea which is good for energy and surprisingly sweet; pur-tea which is compressed like a brick, can be used many times and can keep for up to 20 years and lychee and rose tea, which is very sweet and uses real rosebuds for the aroma.

In the afternoon, we went to the Forbidden City (aka Gugong), home of many former emperors, and this was a real eye-popper, even though it is currently only half-restored. Built during the Ming (1368-1644) and Qing (1644-1911) dynasties, this architectural wonder housed the emperor, empress and imperial concubines and served as a seat for government for more than 500 years.

This walled city is one kilometre long by 750 metres wide and is surrounded by a 52-metre wide moat and 10ft castle-style walls. Jessica explained that in the emperor's time, only he would be allowed to walk through the centre opening of the gate. The other four openings would be used by the empress, the royal servants (all men were eunuchs) and the concubines.

More than one million labourers and 100,000 craftsmen toiled for 14 years to assemble the hundreds of halls, pavilions, libraries, courtyards and gardens that cover the Forbidden City's 180-acre site and today it is open to all.

There are lots of superstitions and symbolism surrounding the Forbidden City. For example, Jessica said all the main buildings were built on a north-south axis with all their doors facing south – because it was believed only bitter winds and barbarians came from the north!

Incredibly, the emperor's bedroom had 27 beds – all occupied at night – so no-one would know which one he was sleeping in and sneak up and murder him!

There was also a whole building for the empress's birthday celebrations, while another building had two rooms – one for weddings and one for human sacrifices, hence perhaps Bring Your Daughter To The Slaughter (apologies to Iron Maiden).

Numbers are hugely important too – eight symbolises the eight noble paths in Buddhism and is thought to be lucky, hence the Olympics started on the 08/08/08, while nine signifies merriment and 25 is a heavenly number (which is why I must be so happy at my house – it is number 25).

On returning to our hotel, I feel as if I have been assaulted by colour today – so many reds, golds, greens and blues at the amazing buildings we have seen, not to mention the cyclists in the rain this morning.

After collecting our Trans-Siberian tickets, which have been delivered to the hotel, we arrange to go to the Chinese opera tomorrow night, email all our friends then take off down Wangfujing Street in search of a top Peking Duck restaurant, which we find in a nearby side-street.

We enjoyed a half duck with pancakes, freshly sliced by the chef at our table, then made our way past Donghuamen Night Market, which is well known for serving up all manner of foods.

The Chinese do eat all sorts of things which would make Brits cringe and I never forget reading Colin Thubron's Behind The Wall, in which he tells of how he saw an owl for sale at a food stall, so he bought it, hid it on the Trans-

Siberian and later released it – much to the disgust of his fellow travellers, who were horrified that he had let such an expensive meal go!

Thankfully there are no owls or other live creatures at Donghuamen Night Market, although we spot plenty of stuffed dumplings and pancakes, kebabs, squid, glazed fruit and other tasty snacks, as well as deep-fried scorpion, crickets, silkworm, octopus and even starfish. We vow to come down here on Friday night to try some 'traditional Beijing street delicacies.'

Exploring on our own

W E are unleashed into the city on our own today. The lovely thing about our travel company, The Russia Experience, is that it specialises in semi-independent travel, so you are not part of a big group and you can build in free days to do what you like.

It is always great to have a good local guide, like Sally and Jessica, but you sometimes feel that you are being shown the city as they would like you to see it, rather than as it really is – warts and all!

After a long, leisurely breakfast, we went out with the aim of going down to Tiananmen Square.

The parks in Beijing are all full of old people enjoying the fresh air and doing Tai Chi or playing Mah-Jong and as we walked down through one park, we saw an old man painting Chinese characters on the pavement in oil. He encouraged us to have a go and although he didn't speak any English, we were able to make our characters look a bit like his and it was all good fun.

We walked a bit further and two Chinese girls stopped us and chatted to us in English and it turned out they were art students and they had an exhibition in a nearby building, so we followed them.

There was some lovely work on display and I did purchase a painting of cranes on silk for approximately £10, which they carefully rolled up and placed in a stout box, so it should be safe to travel in my suitcase for 5,000 miles overland.

We continued on our walk to Tiananmen Square, where we saw the famous portrait of Chairman Mao – though we decided against visiting his mausoleum (big queues!).

I was only 14 at the time of the Tiananmen Square riot in the late 1980s, but I remember the incident well. There is little to remind you of the student deaths here now – indeed today it is full of students meeting each other and gossiping, as well as the brightly-coloured Olympic displays, which are just being dismantled.

We wandered off to the Quimen gate end of the square and headed towards the hutongs nearby. Hutongs are tiny, ancient alleyways packed with doors, which open onto a collection of rooms and spaces that can house up to 20 families. There are no bathrooms in these homes – instead there are public toilet and washroom blocks in every street, which everyone shares.

Although these living spaces appear cramped, the people living here seemed quietly contented with their lot and the hutongs themselves are very clean and tidy – in many places there were even flowers and vegetables growing on trellises or in pots, as well as pigeons and budgies in cages.

One family beckoned us into their home as they sat down to lunch and although not one of them spoke more than a few words of English, they were happy for us to look round and to take their photos.

A little further on, we stumbled upon Lui Li Chang (aka Antique Street), which was full of beautifully painted buildings. It was there that a young man with a charming three-year-old boy said he would take us on a tour of the hutongs on his motorised rickshaw, so we agreed.

He took us on a great trip and showed us family houses with the Chinese sign for double happiness on the doors; a gorgeous boutique hotel called the Spring Garden Hotel; an old bookshop; the mosque and much more.

Each time he stopped, he showed us a card with the name for what we were seeing printed in English, but his little boy was a delight and he spoke quite a few English words, including 'hello' and 'dog'.

When we had first got on the rickshaw and asked the young man how much, he didn't appear to speak English, but had indicated three. Nikki thought it was three yuan, I thought it was more likely to be 30 yuan, but it turned out when we reached Tiananmen Square (he wouldn't take us to where we wanted), it was 300 yuan each.

We didn't have that much on us and I suddenly realised that was more than one of us would pay for the Great Wall tour, so we gave him 350 yuan and left. He didn't call the police or try to come after us and although I felt a bit awkward about it because the tour had been a lot of fun, we agreed he had done quite well really because he had received about £30 for an hour's work.

Sitting down in a nearby cafe with a cool drink, I reflected that the hutongs had been a real eye-opener in more ways than one, but what had struck me most was that although the people in these ancient villages had looked poor to my Western eyes, I had not heard any crying children or raised voices, even though I had been wandering round for several hours there.

What a contrast to our country - walk along any street in Britain during the daytime and you are bound to hear arguing, screaming and shouting within the first ten to 20 minutes!

We headed to the shops in Wanfujing Street and it was there that I noticed several boarded-up areas on the edges of the streets. The boards featured Olympic designs and looked very attractive, but on closer inspection, I realised they were hiding old hutongs, many of which had been partly pulled down.

I had heard the traditional hutongs were fast disappearing to make way for roads, business parks and high-rises and that many had been removed in time for the Olympic Games. I can only wonder at what happened to the inhabitants – where are those families now?

We walked back to our hotel from Wanfujing Street, freshened up, went to a nearby restaurant for another cheap and hugely satisfying dinner and then popped back to Red Wall Hotel to pick up our opera tickets.

The concierge bravely stood in the road in the growing darkness for about 15 minutes to hail us a taxi and then we were off to the Liyuan Theatre, which turned out to be inside a hotel and was attended by scores of mostly Europeans – the most we have see since this trip started.

The opera wasn't quite as Nikki and I had expected, but it was thoroughly entertaining. Chinese opera is quite stylised and the first story was called Goddess Of Heaven Scattering Flowers and was short, but sweet, with one lady singing about her long journey and doing a ribbon dance.

The second story was called Eighteen Arhats Fighting Wu Kong and was a section of a very long tale about the adventures of the Monkey King. Although there was some singing in the first few minutes, much of the opera was wordless and instead involved lots of very acrobatic and amusing fighting.

What was particularly funny was how many Arhats tried to take Monkey's staff – didn't they realise it was magic and according to folklore it would only obey Monkey? The actor playing Monkey had a very expressive face and I found it highly comical. I know they do acrobatics and variety shows at the Liyuan Theatre and I suspect it's the same cast, so they are a very talented bunch. As with everything in Beijing, it's very colourful too.

We caught a taxi back to Red Wall Hotel and walked into the lobby just in time to see the Chinese astronaut being launched. All the hotel staff were really excited and I believe he is the first Chinese astronaut to attempt a moonwalk/spacewalk.

Friday, September 26, 2008

IT is our last full day in Beijing. We woke to the most stunning blue sky. Because it is a flat, dry northern city on the edge of Mongolia, Beijing has beautiful skies and I am told they are bluest in the freezing air of winter. China's old euphemism for itself was Tianxia: 'All beneath the sky' – and on a bright day like today, what an incredible sky!

After a leisurely breakfast, we left the hotel in search of the Lama Temple and the Temple of Confucius, which looked close to each other on the map. It was a bit of a walk through the busy streets, but we soon found the Lama Temple.

I already feel as if I have been assaulted by colour on this trip, but the Lama Temple was another jaw-dropper. The moment we entered the courtyard I was hit by a sense of reverence and serenity – and I'm not even particularly religious.

The majority of Chinese people are Buddhists and in front

of every highly-decorated hall, local people were lighting incense and going through their prayer routines and the whole experience was fascinating.

The temple buildings were once again a myriad of red, gold, blue and green made familiar by other Ming Dynasty places, but it was what was inside them that was so extraordinary.

In every hall there was a young monk in black robes with a red sash, or occasionally an older monk with a yellow sash, requesting that people don't 'burn incense or film' in the halls. I would have liked to have taken photos, but I didn't dare in case I enraged the Buddhist gods.

I don't know how many deities there are in Buddhism, but they were all there. Each hall had three deities in it and there were halls and halls and halls of them to look at. Each deity had piles of fresh fruit and cups of wine in front of them.

Just when I thought I had seen everything, there was one hall with a massive Buddha in it, followed by a second hall with an even bigger Buddha in it. The second Buddha is in the Guinness World Records book as being the biggest Buddha in the world carved out of a single (sandalwood) tree and he is more than 18 metres tall (over 60ft)!

There was also a hall with a massive throne occupied by a very lifelike model of a Lama, plus a display of hundreds of little golden figurines of different deities, which was fascinating – I just wish I knew more about Buddhism.

Afterwards Nikki and I sat in the courtyard for a few minutes and it was just so peaceful – an extraordinarily uplifting experience and a real world away from anything I have ever felt.

We crossed the busy road and followed a narrow lane

to the Confucius Temple, which although beautiful, was a complete contrast in terms of feeling. I don't know much about Confucian thought either, but a very informative museum display showed us that he travelled a lot and tried to persuade people that the key to life was to achieve a balance between different people and between humans and nature, which sounds like an excellent idea to me.

Confucian sayings include: 'Don't do to others what you don't want done to you', and other moral, but sensible statements. I think I rather like the Confucian way – it's seems to be more about believing in yourself and your ability to do what is right.

After the two temples, we continued walking to Beihei Park, which is a large green space and lake in the centre of Beijing, where attractions include the White Dagoda on Jade Island and many temples.

We strolled down the banks in the sunshine, stopped at a lakeside restaurant for juice and ice cream and generally admired the beautiful buildings and scenery. We even saw some mandarin ducks on the lake. A mandarin drake is renowned for his fidelity, as well as his colours. He mates for life, which is why wedding presents in China traditionally include a pair of mandarin ducks.

The top part of Beihei Park near the Bell Tower and the Drum Tower is rickshaw city with hundreds of rickshaw drivers offering to pedal you round the nearby hutongs (known as Beijing's Hutongs). Although pedal-power is authentic, I think we got a much better insight into traditional hutongs yesterday, when we were south of Tiananmen Square.

In the southern part of Beihei Park, you can feast your eyes on more temples and watch people having dancing or exercise sessions, or practising Tai Chi. The Chinese seem to love nothing more than being outside in the fresh air.

From Beihei Park, we went into nearby Jingshan Park (also known as Coal Hill Park), where you can climb to five temples on top of the hill, which give you the most spectacular views of the city.

From the highest temple, you can see from the Forbidden City just below the park right across the modern city and to the mountains beyond. Anything within the second ring road is the old city, while the third, fourth, fifth and sixth ring roads are all in the new city.

Afterwards, we returned to the hotel for a brief rest, before venturing down to Donghuamen Night Market for some street food. In this famous market, the licensed traders cook a wide range of food and it is a classic place for a young Beijing lad to bring his girlfriend for a night out to shock her with his gastronomic bravery by eating scorpions, crickets, grilled snakeskins and other unusual treats on offer.

I couldn't face the fried scorpions and instead feasted on squid, chicken pancake, fried dumplings and a strange greenish juice with dipping doughnuts, which may have been bamboo juice and was very refreshing.

Whilst eating, I noticed a painfully thin young man in the shadows on the edge of the night market. After a while, I realised he was reaching into the bins in search of scraps to eat. His look was unforgettable when he realised I was watching him...

Someone tried to hand him some yuan, but he turned away, too proud to accept charity...

It is a sad thing to see someone starving in a city so buoyant after the Olympics, especially when everyone's mind is full of the lavish closing ceremony and every English person is clapped on the back by Chinese people saying: "Good luck, Britain"; and "London 2012, it's your Olympics next."

All aboard the Trans-Sib

Saturday, September 27, 2008

TODAY we will join the famous Trans-Siberian Railway to start our 5,000-mile journey through northern China, Mongolia, Siberia and Russia.

We got up just before 5am, packed, snacked and left the hotel by 5.40am. A taxi was flagged down for us to take us to the Beijing Central Railway Station to catch our train to the Mongolian capital of Ulaanbaatar.

The station was absolutely heaving with people as we arrived just before 6am. I paid the cab driver and some smartly-dressed chap came up and offered to help carry our cases for us, as there were a lot of steps to negotiate. It seemed like a good idea at the time, though Nikki and I knew he would want money and decided between ourselves to give him a maximum of ten yuan (£1).

Nikki stopped on the top of the footbridge to take a photo of the sunrise and I stayed with the man with the cases. Nikki called to me that she would meet me under the clock tower at the station, so I stopped the chap there, but there was no sign of Nikki.

The man started demanding money and asked for 50 yuan – typing it out on his phone because I didn't understand him. I did all the shaking of my head and pretended I didn't have very much and eventually sent him away with 20 yuan.

There was still no sign of Nikki and I hoped she hadn't run into him. I waited for at least 15 minutes under the first clock tower, then I started to wonder if she meant the second clock tower, so I began pacing between the two with both our cases in tow.

By 6.25am, I decided I had missed her and she must have gone into the terminal, so I joined the queue – and by goodness, was I pushed about! Bearing in mind I had Nikki's suitcase and mine, plus my rucksack and a separate plastic bag full of snacks, I had a very rough time hauling it all through security – I am super-midget at only 5ft 2ins and less than nine stone!

Eventually, I got through and I asked the first guard I saw if he had seen my friend, but he misunderstood, so I went to the police desk and Nikki suddenly appeared behind me. Laughing at how we had managed to miss each other, we went to the platform, posed for photos with the famous train (K23 Beijing-Ulaanbaatar) and found our compartment.

The train was more modern than the guidebooks had led me to believe – it had a shower and the samovar was not urn-like, as in the book, but a modern unit. The provodnitsas (carriage attendants) were dressed like air hostesses, except they had knee-high boots on.

Our compartment was slightly smaller than expected and we had just got in and started eating bananas when three girls came in with tonnes of luggage! We thought two of them must be sleeping in with us, but it turned out only one girl was staying on the train.

Her name was Garig and she told us that she was a nurse from Mongolia, but she had been working in America for 18 months and sending all her money back home. She said she was really looking forward to going home and seeing her daughter, who is now three-and-a-half.

Garig told us lots of things about the Mongolian diet and the fact the country is very poor – and I am sure we will see that. It is a sad fact that more than 80 per cent of Mongolians actually live and work outside the country.

The train departed on time and started to wind its way through the mountains around Beijing and out through northern China.

After a while I went for a walk around the train and discovered it was very long, with 12 passenger carriages before the dining car. Some Canadian train-buffs told me the train was being pulled by a virtually new Chinese electric engine, which was the pride of the fleet.

Some four hours into the journey, I saw the Great Wall of China snaking around the foothills of some mountains in the distance – it's amazing to think this is part of the same structure I climbed in Beijing several hundred miles away.

China itself is a massive country covering some 3,700,000 square miles, including the disputed territory of Tibet, which makes China the third biggest country in the world after Russia and Canada.

During the afternoon the landscape started to change. There were more crops being tilled in small patches, rather than big fields of sweetcorn. In some fields the corn had been hand-cut and bundled into stooks. Many more sheep and cattle were being looked after by herders. I saw a few old Massey-Ferguson style tractors and I even spotted one man using a hand-plough pulled by the unlikely pairing of a donkey and an oxen.

By 5pm – some distance after Xining – the landscape became quite sandy. Nikki and I went down to the dining car to see what was on offer and everything we fancied appeared to be off. We got something completely different to what we tried to order, but we didn't fuss.

After dinner, we returned to our compartment and I did a Spiderman act to climb into the top bunk (there's no ladder as such!) and made my bed – hard to do when you are eight feet up in the roof-space. I went to have a little nap and the next thing I knew, it was around 11pm and we were stopping at the Chinese border town of Erlian, which had an amazing Olympic display outside the station.

An official came round to collect our passports, customs forms and departure cards and then the provodnitsas shooed us off the train and we were released into the terminal without our documentation while they took the train away to have the bogies (wheels) changed. This process takes hours, but has to be done because the track in Mongolia and Russia is a different width to that in China!

We went into the station shop to change our remaining yuan into Mongolian tugrik (or tug) and I handed over 140 yuan and got 23,800 tug back! A quick sniff of the banknotes also confirmed the rumour that Mongolian money does indeed smell of sheep!

Incredibly the guards even let us into the town of Erlian for a stroll (passport-less!) and lots of Mongolian people poured into the last Chinese shop before the border to stock up on food and drink because it is cheaper here than in Mongolia.

When we eventually got back on the train, it was a short journey to the Mongolian border (no – the two borders are not the same), where we were asked for our passports and forms again and detained for almost another two hours.

Altogether we have spent more than four hours at the

borders tonight and although we had effectively lost an hour because we crossed a time zone coming into Mongolia, we still didn't get to bed until after 2am.

Sunday, September 28, 2008

I WAS the first one awake, so I snuck out of the compartment in my pyjamas and was amazed to find great vistas of sand in front of me – the Gobi! I was jolted awake when we had stopped at Sainshand at around 5.20am and had dozed off again briefly, so I decided this must be the very edges of the desert.

When Marco Polo reached the edge of the Gobi Desert, a daunting sight confronted him – a stark, empty wasteland which locals warned him he would need a year or more to cross. Skirting the southern edge of the desert, the 13th Century traveller and his party were terrified of its dramatic mirages, or evil spirits as they called them, which easily lured people to their deaths.

But they kept their heads and eventually reached the safety of Kublai Khan's summer palace at Shangdu, near the modern town of Duolun.

The Gobi is Asia's largest desert and covers an incredible 500,000 square miles of northern China and southern Mongolia. Its terrain varies from flat, stony plains to undulating sand dunes; from sparse grasslands to mountains more than 12,000ft high. The climate is desperately harsh: in some areas rainfall is less than three inches a year and temperatures can range from minus 40 deg C in winter to more than 43 deg C in summer. No other desert on Earth experiences such extreme variations.

Remarkably, in spite of these conditions, some areas of the Gobi support wildlife including antelope, gazelle, wild asses, sand grouse and vipers. In certain areas, there is even sufficient grass for Mongol nomads to graze their herds of camel, sheep and horses.

I was soon transfixed by the rolling landscape and startling bright, cloudless skies – no wonder they call Mongolia the 'Land Of Blue Sky'. I sat in a corridor window-seat watching the landscape slowly becoming greener and herds of two-humped Bactrian camel, sheep, goats and horses go by, as well as the odd ger (a round Mongolian tent), some herdsmen and hawks.

Before Buddhism was brought to Mongolia, the ancient Mongolians worshipped Tengri – the spirit of the blue horizon. Mountains and high places were sacred because it was there you could be closest to Tengri's sky kingdom. It was easy to feel quite spiritual watching this great land unfolding before me.

I was joined by my compartment members in due course and we rolled into Choyr at about 9.15am – time for a stroll along the station. I grabbed my camera to take some photos of the provodnitsas cleaning the carriage windows and some of the beautifully-dressed Mongolian ladies serving tea on the platform. But I was soon accosted by two endearing boys with a boxful of crystals, which turned out to be colourful fluoride crystals.

I love crystals and I was looking for the very best green and purple-banded one, so the boys searched right through their box to find the right one for me. I told them I would give them each some money if I could take their picture too and at first they seemed unsure, but when they saw I was offering them American dollars (USD), rather than tugrik, they were excited.

I took the picture and gave them one dollar each – our

Canadian friends said that was extravagant, but the two boys were lovely.

Back on the train, I folded up my bedding, in the loosest sense of the words because I haven't mastered bed-making on the move yet. A fellow Mongolian traveller pointed out a few tahki, Mongolia's wild horse, which is also known at Przewalski's horse. This is an extremely rare animal instantly recognisable by its sandy colour, dark legs and silver and black stand-up mane.

I know there is a conservation project to breed them within Mongolia's Hustai National Park, but I had no idea there may be some tahki lookalikes in the wild. I feel extremely privileged to have seen one outside a zoo.

The other thing about Mongolia, apart from its completely different landscape, is its altitude. The carriages have an electronic display board, which is telling us we are regularly travelling at higher than 1,200 metres. The highest we reached was about 1,700 metres around an hour from Ulaanbaatar. Not long afterwards, I was amazed to see an old steam engine pulling a large freight train behind us.

Coming into Ulaanbaatar, the city seems to be a complete hotch-potch spread out over some distance, but what was immediately obvious was the colour. It would seem every last house is painted a different colour and there are loads of gers all mixed in with the houses, again with brightly-painted doors.

On arrival in Ulaanbaatar, Garig gave a huge smile and started waving to her little daughter on the platform and the next moment, loads of Mongolians piled onto the train to help their relatives and friends off, so we were nearly squashed in the rush!

A quick search of the platform unearthed our guide

Tseegii (which sounds a bit like Jackie), who is 22 and super-cheerful. She leads us to a Russian jeep and driver and they take us to the nearby Flower Hotel for a chance to freshen up in the hot and cold plunge pools, before heading off for the 55km drive to the ger camp, which is situated on a massive plain surrounded by mountains.

Elstei is described as a tourist ger camp and I soon discovered why – between April and October it has showers with hot water for a few hours and flushing toilets. In addition, there is a nice warm clubhouse/restaurant with an excellent chef. But the biggest surprise was the gers themselves – we expected to be sharing with other people and have beds on the floor, but no, when the door opened there was a colourfully decorated ger for two with proper beds, an electric light and even lounge chairs and a power-point. Words cannot express the shock of having this lovely unit to ourselves!

Tseegii brought us some tea and bread and butter, then it had been arranged that we should do some archery, but it was too windy and so we asked if we could go for a walk to the top of the nearest hill and everyone agreed that was a good idea, so we set off – completely free in this wild country.

We went past a herd of horses near the gers of a nomad family and continued up the steep hillside to the top, where there was a cairn. During our jeep ride, Tseegii had explained Mongolian tradition states that when you find an oovu, or sacred cairn, you should walk round it three times in a clockwise direction, throw a stone on it and make a wish.

From the top of the hill there were outstanding views to the Chingghis (Genghis) Khan memorial and right across the plains and mountains. I don't think I have ever experienced such a huge sense of space as I have here.

We returned to camp and Tseegii and I got to pet the foal, who had been tied up so his mum could be milked for koumiss (fermented mares' milk). Then we went into the restaurant as it was getting dark and played the Mongolian horseracing game with sheep's knuckle bones. These bones, I later learned can be used for fortune-telling too.

We were joined by Pat from South Wales and Rachel from New York and the game involved throwing four sheep knuckle bones and moving your steed according to the number of times your bones landed on the 'horse' side. Alas, I was on the slowest horse.

Dinner was a rather international affair with salad, pancake rolls and steamed ginger cake. Afterwards, Rachel and Pat kept us amused with their travel tales. Pat is 79 and has been to Madagascar and much of the USA and was returning from the Beijing Paralympics, where she had been watching her daughter competing, while Rachel is returning overland after spending some time in South Korea.

By about 8.30pm we retired to our ger and a young Mongolian girl came in to fire up the wood-burning stove for us. She said that if we wanted to leave the door unlocked, she would come back in at around 7am and re-stoke the fire for us and although this may sound dicey, the camp is well-guarded and everyone else does it, because it means the ger is warm when you get out of bed in the morning!

I have always wanted to come to Mongolia, which is described by Lonely Planet as being one of the last unspoilt travel destinations in Asia. It really is a marvellous country, but my only worry is that my mobile phone cannot pick up a signal here, so I will not be able to text Mum or Hugh for several days.

Magical Mongolia

Monday, September 29, 2008.

THE guidebooks describe Ulaanbaatar as the coldest capital city in the world and I think they could be right – it is freezing outside this morning and there is a heavy frost on top of our ger.

I was awoken by the sound of horses neighing and our resident ger rodent squeaking. It scuttles out from behind the beds from time to time and it is brown and kind of gerbil-like and very, very cute.

We went up to the washroom and Nikki braved the showers – I might do this later this afternoon when it might still be a few degrees above freezing!

On returning to our ger, we found it was toasty-warm and the fire was well alight. One of the most impressive things about Mongolia is the complete silence – you can really get away from it all here.

We went out for a little walk and took some photos before breakfast, which included hot dumplings, milk, tea, pastries and samosas – our chef is Indian and believes that the Mongolian diet is too full of fat for most visitors to handle because it is rich in meat and dairy products, so he prefers to serve a wide mix of dishes, together with more Mongolian specialities like the dumplings.

Tseegii reported that it had been quite cold last night and had dropped to minus 10 deg C. We are still very high up too – Ulaanbaatar is 1,350 metres above sea level and the steppes we are on are a little higher still.

After breakfast, we had a little time to ourselves and then I went off riding with Tseegii, while Nikki went walking. As a horse-owner and experienced rider, it has long been an ambition of mine to ride a Mongolian horse and I wasn't disappointed.

They may be small – my Mongolian horse was no more than 13hh – but they are very tough and fast. The bridles are similar to ours, while the saddle has a back-cinch like a Western saddle, plus more shape than an English saddle to sit in, but less padding, so it pays to have a bum hardened by many hours on horseback like I have!

I joined a larger group of riders and we watched the herd of horses being corralled and then singled out and caught with a lasso on the end of a long cane. These horses – though well-trained for the saddle – roam semi-wild, so you cannot just walk up and catch one with a headcollar or bridle, like we do in England.

They have no shoes on their feet and have woolly coats and very long manes – I am reminded of a poem Nikki told me about, which was written by her friend Linda Lamus. In the poem, Linda describes her Mongolian horse as: 'rugged, long-bodied and low-slung' and the horse tells her that if she should fall, he will rein her in fast and plait her in his mane. It's a very striking image.

The Mongolian horses don't have names and as it is quite a large herd, they are usually referred to by their colour. Mine was a chestnut horse with a flaxen (blond) mane and tail, known to everyone as Yellow.

Mongolian horses are also slightly different to ride in that they steer more like a Western horse and the way to make them go forward is to say: "Chu!" But according to Tseegii, almost everyone who visits Mongolia wants to ride the horses – even if they have never ridden before.

Although we left Elstei Ger Camp in one big group, Tseegii and I were soon taken off on our own by one of the Mongolian herdsmen, who rode using a traditional wooden saddle, which was highly decorated. We trotted and cantered across the steppes and I soon found Yellow was remarkably sure-footed and was keen to go on at all times – if a little flighty at ditches and peculiar-looking things.

We rode across to the recently-built Genghis Khan Monument and I was somewhat awe-struck as I stood in front of the great warrior's silver statue, riding a horse descended from his horse in his beautiful country.

Few Eastern races can have experienced such great swings of fortune as the Mongols. At the beginning of the 13th Century they could hardly be called a nation: rather a collection of scattered nomadic tribes led by bickering warlords.

But within decades they had united under the inspiring leadership of Genghis Khan to establish the greatest empire the world had ever known. By 1242, the Mongols had pushed south into China and westwards into Russia, Poland and Austria, until almost a third of the known world lay at their feet.

In 1279, Genghis's grandson Kublai Khan completed his family's conquest of China, but less than a century later the Mongols' power was on the wane – and in 1368 they were driven back across the frontier. Some 300 years on, they were themselves conquered by the Chinese and their territory was divided into two regions, Outer and Inner Mongolia.

Outer Mongolia won its independence in the 1920s, but it became a virtual protectorate of communist Russia and was only truly a free country from 1990 onwards, while Inner Mongolia (capital: Hohhot) has remained a province of China – the country's fifth largest.

In both parts of Mongolia, communism has brought many changes to the inhabitants' traditional nomadic way of life. In Inner Mongolia in particular, where the Han Chinese greatly outnumber the Mongols themselves, the authorities have succeeded in forcing many of the population to live on farms or in towns.

But in the great open steppes of the region, many ancient customs have survived, often unchanged by the centuries: herdsmen and their families can still be found living in gers and gather with other families to enjoy open air dances and the traditional sports of wrestling, archery and horse-racing.

Naadam is the biggest holiday in the Mongolian calendar and is the festival of the 'three manly sports' – wrestling, archery and horsemanship. Under communism, Naadam was adapted and a modern version can be seen in Ulaanbaatar.

For a more traditional Naadam festival, visit Sainshand in the southern Gobi. Naadam takes place over a few days in July and includes an opening ceremony, the three manly sports and the unusual sport of target-shooting with anklebones!

Sat in the shadow of the Genghis Khan Monument drinking Mongolian cola and playing with a local nomad's puppy, with my Mongolian horse grazing nearby, I felt I was almost drowning in history.

We rode a different way home and for a two-hour ride

they charged just $10 USD (about £5). It was also great to get the saddles off, let the horses go and watch them go straight back to the herd – magic to think of them as one big family!

Mongolia is very much a land of horses – indeed horses outnumber people within the country. For centuries people have raised horses to ride and produce milk and they treat their horses like their closest friends.

It is therefore only natural that many songs, poems and stories have been written in praise of the horse. Legend has it that the most quintessential of Mongolian musical instruments, the morin huur or horse-head fiddle, was designed by a young man who – grieving at the death of his favourite horse – carved an instrument in the dead animal's likeness and made strings from its mane.

Next it was lunch, which is the biggest meal of the day in Mongolia. Then we walked across the steppe to the opposite side of the valley to visit some of the local nomad gers, where we met with the father of one of the girls who works at the camp.

The ger itself was beautifully decorated with lots of exquisite embroidery and it turns out it is the daughter – who is in her early 20s – who does all of it, although her mother, who died two years ago, was also very good at embroidery.

Over a cup of 'suutei tsai' or salty tea, which is actually nicer than it sounds, plus bread and butter and a cheese scone-like product made with curd, we talked for much of the afternoon.

It turns out the daughter is about to be married and leave the family ger and her dad, who is 65, will be left at home with the youngest brother, who is 20. The father has seven children in total and his eldest son now lives in Chicago. The father plans to visit Chicago next summer and his dream is to drive a car in America! We all laugh at this and I tell him he is very brave.

He has a television and DVD in his ger, which is solar-powered and he also regularly emails his son in Chicago from Ulaanbaatar. He even tends his stock on a motorbike! It was great to talk to him and his daughter and after we left, Tseegii said it was the first time she had seen him smile since his wife died.

On returning to our own ger camp, we had a go at Mongolian archery with moderate success. I hit the target a couple of times – I suspect Genghis must have bestowed his special powers on me when I gazed at his memorial this morning, because I normally can't hit anything! We also saw just how quickly a Mongolian ger can be taken down and re-erected. The ger really is an incredible structure and is formed with waterproof canvas as a top layer and warm woollen blanket as an inside layer, stretched over wooden lattice-style ribs and all tied up and anchored down with plaited horsehair ropes.

In the evening I sat down to write, all the time watching the horses outside. I saw the couple who milk the mares returning with their bucket and I asked if I could take a look – it does indeed look like cow's milk, but when they indicated I could taste, I found it was very sweet and still warm.

Tseegii told me a little bit about how temperatures can change by more than 37 deg C in one day, and she also spoke about the Great Zud - the winters of 1999/00 and 2001/02, which were particularly severe in Mongolia.

They were the coldest and longest winters in living memory. Zud is a Mongolian word meaning any condition that stops livestock getting to grass – in this case heavy snowfall and impenetrable ice cover.

After three seasons of bad winter conditions, the livestock population in Mongolia plummeted from 33 million to 24 million and in the worst hit areas, the nomads lost between a quarter and half their livestock, which is their only source of income, food, fuel and security.

Considering this only happened a few years ago, I am amazed at how this country has picked itself up and got on with life – whilst still presenting good humour and hospitality to its visitors.

Dinner was Mongolian barbecue, which consists of melt-in-the-mouth mutton, served with rice and lots of cooked vegetables and salad. We sat on a table with a Japanese gentleman and his guide and as Tseegii speaks Japanese too, there was soon a spectacular three-way conversation going on.

Our chef came out to tell us a little bit about the food and explained to me how he boiled the mutton over hot stones with a little water, plus some salt, pepper and garlic, then the vegetables are added a little before the end and cooked through with the meat.

After the Mongolian barbecue, we decided we must try Mongolian vodka before we leave and I have today developed a streaming nose, so we thought – kill or cure!

We bought a whole bottle of Mongolian vodka and between Nikki, the Japanese chap and I, we proceeded to drink it during the evening, as well as buying our guides beer or soft drinks. We retired to our ger at about 10pm and it was toasty-warm as the fire had been lit some hours before. It wasn't difficult to get to sleep.

To Ulaanbaatar

Tuesday, September 30, 2008

I MUST see a Mongolian sunrise before I leave the steppes. I got out of bed shortly after 6.15am and stepped into the eerie light outside, where it was definitely below zero.

There was not a soul to be seen except the camp dog and the mare and foal.

Even with several layers of clothes on, I knew I would just freeze if I sat down, so I started to walk in a roundabout circle, because if I went too close to the camp, the dog would start to bark.

It was absolutely total silence out on the steppe – the cleanest and most perfect silence I have ever heard. I took a couple of pre-dawn photographs and then watched as the sun crept over the skyline just a few minutes after seven. I took a perfect shot, but in another second the sun was up fully and the opportunity was lost. Mongolian sunrises differ from those at home or in Beijing in that there is no cloud, so it is just one big rush of golden light.

I walked back to the camp in a roundabout way, taking care not to disturb the camp dog. When I stepped back into Ger 3 (Mongolian lucky number, apparently) Nikki was still in bed, so I stoked up the fire well.

Breakfast was once again a tasty affair with pastries and

wild berry jam and after breakfast, we said our goodbyes and left the ger camp for the drive back to Ulaanbaatar. Nearing the city, I got a text message from Hugh to tell me that not only has he started doing emails, but he had got broadband too. I am really impressed!

Arriving in the city is a huge contrast to the peace and quiet of the ger camp. Tseegii takes us to the Bayangol Hotel, which is a pleasant four-star, but is a bit tatty in places. Our room has got the tiniest bath I have ever seen – it is a squeeze even for a midget like me!

Nikki and I go to the hotel's business centre to do our emails and I write a post for the blog, then we go back to our room for a snack, before meeting Tseegii for an afternoon city tour.

We went to Sukhbaatar Square, which is thought to be the biggest square in the world and seemed even bigger than Tiananmen Square. It is named after Damdin Sukhbaatar who was known as the hero of the revolution and declared Mongolia's final independence from the Chinese in July 1921. The square now bears his name and a large statue of him on a horse to remind people that he rode to Moscow in seven days to seek Lenin's assistance in shaking off the Chinese.

The words he apparently proclaimed at the time are engraved at the bottom of the statue and read: "If we, the whole people, unite in our common effort and common will, there will be nothing in the world that we cannot achieve, that we will not have learnt or failed to do."

As we turned away from Sukhbaatar's statue, we came face to face with Parliament House, built as every good ger is – facing south. Flying proudly on top of the government building was the Mongolian national flag, the blue and red soyombo, which symbolises freedom and independence.

Next was the State Department Store, which was opened in 1924 and sells everything! Tseegii led us up to the fifth floor to browse in the Mongolian souvenir section and I love the colourful dels (traditional coats), but can't quite justify the purchase.

We were walking through the streets on our way to the Gandan Monastery when a man approached us. He tried to talk to Nikki first and Tseegii tried to speak to him and we thought he had gone away.

But then I felt the shoulder strap of my rucksack being pulled quite hard and I spun round, placed my hand on the front of his shoulder in a 'stopping' motion and said loudly: "No". I think he understood because he left us alone, but I am still not sure whether he thought he could get my rucksack off of me, or whether he was just trying to steer me into his shop!

Many Mongolians are poor – indeed one-third live below the poverty line, but unlike most other countries, this does not necessarily mean that people are going hungry and I didn't notice anyone begging in the streets as we walked through Ulaanbaatar.

Most people in Mongolia live a healthy, robust life even if they have been out of work for years. This is because of the strong family network. One family member with a decent job has the responsibility to support his or her family and distribute his wealth among siblings.

It was the rail route that created Ulaanbaatar as we know it today – before the railway, the Mongolian capital wasn't even fixed in one place, but followed the Royal Court and its retinue in ger tents around a calendar route of Mongolia's Buddhism monasteries.

The most important of the monasteries, Gandantegchinlen

(known as Gandan in everyday speech) was where the Royal Court spent the long, snowbound winters. It was only when Sukhbaatar wanted to enlist Lenin's help in overthrowing the Chinese that the USSR decided to build a railway to its new Asian ally and Mongolia became the second country in the world to join what was known as the 'great experiment in socialism'.

The Gandan Monastery turned out to be absolutely beautiful and although I am sure there should have been an admission fee, there was no-one there to collect one. There were hundreds of pigeons in the courtyard and the main hall had a massive Buddha in it, as well as the figurines of 800 other deities and lots and lots of prayer wheels.

Next door in what was called the Women's Monk's Ger, two young girls were singing Om Mani Padme Hum (May Happiness Prevail) in preparation for an examination. Their grandmother, who was beautifully dressed in traditional Mongol style, was also sitting there proudly watching and she allowed us to take photos of her and the girls.

Mongolia is a very religious nation and historically the nomads believed in shamanism – a form of mysticism – which has co-existed and intermixed with Buddhism for centuries. Shamanism is based around the shaman, who is called a 'bo' if male or 'udgan' if female and has special medical and religious powers.

One of the shaman's main functions is to cure any sickness caused by the soul straying, and to accompany the soul of a dead person to the other world. Shamans act as intermediaries between the human and spirit worlds and communicate with spirits during trances – which can last up to six hours.

Today, few Mongolians follow Shamanism and instead

most practice the yellow sect of Buddhism, which came from Tibet in the 14th Century.

After the Gandan Monastery, we weaved our way through the white stupas to the temple next door, which was beautiful and had a 'Magic Tree' where people make wishes. Tseegii explained the legend states that the area used to be heavily forested and there was a great fire, but the magic tree was the only one which didn't burn down, so now people consider it to be lucky.

On closer inspection, I saw the truck was full of matches that people had pushed into the cracks as if to say: "Ha ha, you can't burn me!"

We were just walking back to the hotel when we saw Pat, who said she had thoroughly enjoyed exploring the city and that she and Rachel would be catching the train for Irkutsk tonight. We wouldn't catch up with them again and so we said our goodbyes.

Nikki and I went up to our room to freshen up and we had a beer before going out to dinner. We didn't fancy going far, so we popped round the corner to the Grand Khaan Irish Pub. It was absolutely heaving with people, but we only had to wait 15 minutes before a table was found for us.

After perusing the somewhat international menu for some time, Nikki chose Singapore Chicken, while I had the Mongolian beef hotpot, plus a large cup of hot cranberry juice in an attempt to kill my cold. Then we returned to the hotel for an early night.

Wednesday, October 1, 2008

ON waking this morning, I discovered my streaming nose had dried out a bit! We went down to breakfast, which proved to be an extremely good buffet with plenty of variation.

Nikki went to check her emails quick, while I returned to our room to pack, as we are supposed to be checking out at noon. Nikki had booked a massage for 10am, so she popped back to the room briefly to grab a few things, then left to go to the massage room.

The next thing I knew, there was a knock at the door and it was the massage girl, who was indicating that the massage should take place in the room. I couldn't make her understand it is my friend who wants the massage and she has gone out, so I took her back to reception, who explain to her what has happened and tell me the massage room is on the third floor – so we go up there and find Nikki.

Nikki and the girl then went back to our room, which left me hanging about for an hour, so I located the hotel's shop and found some souvenirs – a sheep knucklebone game, a painting of horsemen on fabric and the most fabulous photo-book about Mongolia in English. The book was expensive, but worth it – it's a long-lasting reminder of the beauty of this extraordinary country and has lots of photos of places we haven't visited.

I read the latest Mongol Messenger newspaper, and also spotted a collection box for an Ulaanbaatar orphanage, so I popped into the business centre to look it up on the internet, and to do my emails. Unfortunately the website for the Lotus Centre had not been updated recently and I couldn't find any address or map to clarify exactly where it was in the city.

I flicked through the guidebook for other ideas for places to visit today, as our train didn't leave until the evening. On rejoining Nikki, we decide to visit the Bogd Khan Winter Palace and the hotel receptionist kindly called us a taxi and told the driver where we wanted to go.

Built between 1893 and 1903, the Winter Palace is the place where Mongolia's eighth living Buddha and last king Jebtzun Damba Hutagt VIII – aka Bogd Khan – lived for 20 years. Somehow the palace escaped destruction by the Russians and has been turned into a museum, which has been described by many as having a haunting atmosphere.

Unfortunately when we got there, the Winter Palace was shut! The driver didn't speak much English, but we managed to convey to him that we wanted to visit Zaisan Hill on the outskirts of the city, which has a massive Buddha on it.

He waited for us while we photographed the huge Buddha, which gazes across the crazy patchwork of Ulaanbaatar, and then he took us back to our hotel. From there, we decided to walk through the city centre to see if we could find the Dashchoylin Monastery.

I think the funny thing about Mongolian people is that they are Asian by ethnicity, but Western by culture. Tseegii has often commented that she doesn't like the Chinese and that Mongolian people are nothing like the Chinese and I am beginning to think it is true. Yesterday we saw people playing pool on a full-sized pool table at the side of the main street – pool is definitely a Western thing, though it is the first time I have seen a pool game played on a pavement!

While the Chinese regularly use their mobile phones, they always seem to make quick to-the-point calls, whereas the Mongolians sit and chat for ages, like we do. Chinese streets are filled with bicycles, while Mongolian streets are choked with cars and it is easy to get run over. This Westernisation of the Mongolians could be the European influence with which their Russian masters immersed them in the 20th Century, or perhaps the long hours many now spend glued to the internet, CNN or MTV.

Dashchoylin Monastery took us a little while to find because it was off the main street, nestled in amongst the Soviet-style tower blocks! But it was a veritable oasis of calm in a busy city and was Tibetan in style, rather than Chinese like the Gandan Monastery. It was sadly covered in peeling paint, but it was a real working monastery because we could hear the young monks chanting.

I think there is something incredibly awe-inspiring about the devotion to religion and the incredible sense of peace at these old monasteries, even though I am not religious myself. I am also constantly surprised by just how friendly Mongolian people are and although we have been warned that Ulaanbaatar is a rough city, we feel at ease in the streets.

On leaving the monastery, we found our way back to Chingghis Khan Avenue amidst the jumble of brightly-coloured buildings and went to the Museum of Natural History, which is packed with dinosaur remains found in the Gobi and all manner of stuffed animals, plus lots of information about the different flora and fauna found in Mongolia. Many of the exhibits had English explanations and it was a fascinating display.

After that, we went down the road to the Museum of National History, where we stopped for a cup of tea and a chocolate bar before going into the exhibition.

Again it was fascinating, with sections taking us from early times in Mongolia right through to the present day. There was even a movie or documentary being shot in the room with the ger, which was causing a lot of fuss, plus a room full of extraordinary regional costumes and jewellery.

What struck me most was just how far Mongolia has come, politically and socially, in the last 20 years – it really is an exciting time for this incredibly friendly and beautiful country.

We left the museum at about 5.30pm and went back to the hotel, where we went into the Casablanca Bar/Restaurant for dinner and I chose my last truly Mongolian meal – Mongolian noodles with mutton.

After dinner, we browsed in the hotel shop, bought a few extra provisions, visited the business centre to make a last check for incoming emails and then met with Tseegii and the minibus, which took us to the train station.

Tseegii gave us a little present each (knucklebones!) and we gave her an envelope containing a tip, because she has been brilliant. She explained that she didn't want to walk home in the dark, so she left us just before we boarded the Irkutsk train.

I was just shoving all my stuff onto the top bunk when our fellow compartment-sharers arrived – Amanda from Gosport and Tracey, the Australian guide whom Nikki had met on the Beijing train.

So here we all were and we were soon pretty comfortable – except for the heat. It was unbearably hot on the train, which was considerably less modern than the Beijing one. We tried to ask for the heating to be turned down, but nothing happened. Some of the men in a nearby compartment asked for a window to be opened, but the provodnitsa indicated that it would be too cold.

It was then that I remembered Hugh's triangular gas key, which I had begged to borrow after I read somewhere that they can be used to open the train's doors and windows. I unearthed it and handed it to the guys to see if they could work out how to undo a window.

They did and they showed us how to do our compartment

window too. We eased it down a fraction of an inch and it was bliss – although we knew we would have to close it before bedtime, or we would all freeze overnight!

The provodnitsas in this carriage have already given us tea/coffee and insisted it is free, so I really don't want to upset them and we have all vowed to be really careful about using the key. (Tracey the Australian guide – who has been on the Trans-Sib at least eight times – is in awe and now she wants a key!)

Onwards to Siberia

Thursday, October 2, 2008.

HAVING gone to bed at about 11pm, I took to sleeping with just a sheet because it was far too warm. Overnight, the train has climbed through the mountainous edges of Mongolia to the border.

Few people realise that Mongolia is about three times the size of France, twice as big as Texas and almost as large as Queensland in Australia.

Until the 20th Century, the country was almost twice its present size and owned a large part of Siberia, which has since been snatched back and is now securely controlled by the Russians.

During the night, the train stopped a number of times and tooted to let other pass, before rolling into the border station of Suhbaatar (also often spelt Suhkbaatar) at around 5.35am, where it stopped for several hours.

I stepped out onto the station at about 7.15am and went to the washroom to freshen up. As I was mooching around on the platform, I realised we weren't a train at all, but just two carriages standing on the track – which looked really odd.

There was nothing much happening on the station except for one old guy wandering around asking people if they wanted to change money – I felt this probably wasn't a good idea as we were unsure of what was a good rate.

By 8am there were lots of Mongolians waiting to get on the train and I switched my mobile on and received a nice message from Tseegii, who said she hoped we had caught the right train and were having a nice time.

I sent her a reply and then picked up my well-browsed copy of Bryn Thomas's Trans-Siberian Handbook to read while I waited for the border crossing to take place.

The crossing seemed to take forever. We had lots of paperwork to fill in, none of which we could read, which made it rather difficult. Luckily Tracey had a bit of an idea about how the different documents are filled in. It was only when I started counting all my various currencies that I realised I had far more tugrik than I thought I did – uh-oh!

Tracey said you couldn't use or change tugrik in Russia, while Amanda told me roughly what the rate of exchange should be. We called the provodnitsa, who helped me catch the attention of the chap who changes money. Under the watchful eyes of the provodnitsa and a border guard, I changed 22,500 tug for 450 roubles (which was a pretty good deal). So I then had six currencies on me, US dollars, UK sterling, a few Chinese yuan, a tiny amount of Mongolian tug, euros and now roubles – and I was very confused.

As well as money-changing activities, there were lots of traders prowling round the train trying to sell (or at least hide) slippers, jeans, socks, tracksuit bottoms and warm jumpers. One lady was trying desperately to make another take a few jumpers – I guess she was concerned that she had too many and the border authorities would take them off of her.

I am quite sorry to leave Mongolia because it is a fabulous

country. It is an ancient land with present-day traditions that are unchanged from the previous millennia.

However, it is also a young country that only gained its independence in 1990 and elected a new government last month. I think we saw the country's new leader coming out of the back of Parliament House when we passed yesterday, because there were lots of smartly-suited officials and the television cameras were following a man dressed in an elegant silver-grey del, who got into a black jeep. He was surrounded by people with bouquets of flowers, which suggests he was a VIP.

But now we speed onwards to Siberia. After a lot of hanging around on the Mongolian border, we had to cross through no man's land before reaching the monster fence which marked the Russian border.

During this time, we had to fill in yet more paperwork and guards came into our compartments and searched our baggage and checked under the beds and up in the roof-space for stowaways. This was all very amusing, especially when they were shown the huge cake being kept cool under the floor, which belongs to one of the men in a nearby compartment.

The guards let us have our passports back and released us into the border town of Naushki, where we were stopped for about two hours. There isn't much in Naushki, just a lot of painted houses on dusty unmade roads, cattle milling loose in the park, a war memorial, a cafe and two little shops.

Nikki and I had a good mooch round and bought some soft drinks, bananas and a small piece of cheese at one of the shops, then took a look at the clothes market and went back to the station, where we hung around for a while and watched railway staff shunting trains back and forth and adding more carriages to our train.

We rejoined our train and after two hours at Naushki, we were off on our way through the Siberian countryside. Hello Russia!

Think Siberia and you are probably thinking of Siberian countryside thick with snow, Dr Zhivago, gulags and fur hats. But on a bright autumn day like today, it is full of 'fall' colours and more reminiscent of Canada or New England, with orange and yellow trees, blue rivers and big mountains.

Siberia itself was not originally Russian territory. It was settled by the Russians from the 15th Century onwards, primarily to prevent the Mongols and Tartars from re-establishing themselves. Later, the Russians kept hold of it purely for reasons of territorial expansion and a drive for the warm water trading ports of the Pacific.

The name of Siberia isn't Russian either – it is thought to come from 'Sebiyr', which means The Sleeping Land in Tartar. Incredibly, Russia was once subject to Siberian rule. From 1240 to 1480, Russia was a subject state of the Mongols and their rule was policed locally for them by the Tartars – a people native to Siberia – who settled in Kazan.

People also have the idea that Siberia is permanently covered in snow, but it's not. Siberia has blazing hot summers with average July/August temperatures of 26-28 deg C, so forest fires can be a real problem.

But the winters are viciously cold and Siberia is thought to be the coldest place on Earth – even colder than the poles – because of its elevation and distance from the ocean. In the north of Siberia, extreme winter lows of minus 62 deg C have been recorded and as low as minus 52 deg C has been recorded in the cities.

All of Siberia lies in Asia and the western borders are

marked by the Ural Mountains, the southern borders are marked by the Altai Mountains (which we crossed early this morning) and the eastern borders by the Sayan Mountains. These mountain ranges effectively make an amazing atmospheric dam that contains the freezing air and keeps Siberia cold in winter.

The other things I have already noticed about Siberia is that everyone has a dog and it is also Lada city – I have a special affection for Ladas because I learned to drive in one and I always thought they were great budget motoring (and pretty reliable too).

This afternoon the gentle motion of the train lulled me to sleep for a while and when I woke, I was surrounded by gorgeous countryside, with mountains and birch trees on one side and a massive lake on the other side. Someone said it was called Goose Lake, though I am not sure if that's right.

We watched the sun go down, tingeing the sandy-coloured tundra fiery red. There's no dining car on this particular leg of the journey, so we joined the great masses in eating noodle soup, a locally-produced pot-noodle type thing, plus the cheese and crackers.

We have an amazing girl from Holland in our carriage. She decided to cycle from home to Beijing to watch some friends competing in the Olympic Games in August. So she has taken five months to go from Holland through Germany, Austria, the Czech Republic, Hungary, Croatia, Serbia, Bulgaria, Turkey, Iran, Turkmenistan, Uzbekistan, Kazahkstan and into China. On the way back, she has also visited Mongolia and is headed back to Moscow and possibly St Petersburg.

Tonight, we are headed towards Ulan Ude, which we

should reach between 9pm and 10pm. Ulan-Ude (pronounced Ulan Uday) is the capital of Buryatia, a semi-autonomous region of Siberia. The Buryats are one of the native Asiatic peoples of Siberia and their ancestors lived here long before Russian settlers came from the west.

Buryat life was nomadic, like most of the steppe people of Siberia and central Asia. The Buryats would rotate from a winter stockade where they would spend the worst winter months to two or three different summer grazing locations.

Cossacks settled in Ulan-Ude from the 17th Century onwards, so today the city is full of Russian settlers and the Buryats are still largely nomadic.

We stopped briefly at Ulan-Ude and the temperature outside when I jumped down onto the platform was a mild 4 deg C. If you have time to look around Ulan Ude, the most popular things to visit are the giant Lenin head and the Ivolginsky Datsan, which is the centre of Buddhism in Russia.

Alas, we weren't staying and there was nothing much happening on the platform, so I jumped back on the train and packed everything up because we are scheduled to get off quite early at Irkutsk in the morning and I plan to be totally organised.

Friday, October 3, 2008.

AS suspected, the carriage attendants woke us up at about 6.45am and made us strip our beds as soon as possible and give back our hand towels. Nikki and I managed a quick snack before the train stopped at Irkutsk at around 8am.

Our new guide Sergei was waiting almost right outside our carriage as we disembarked. We followed him through the station - which had lots of steps - and into the car park where our driver, Valery, was waiting. We popped our cases in the car and began the 120km drive to Bolshoe Goloustnoe, a remote village on the edge of Lake Baikal.

Nikki was soon asleep on the drive, but I was astounded by the amazing colour of the trees as we drove through the frost-sharp Siberian countryside.

We stopped part-way through the route for a short break and there were 'wish trees' where people had tied short pieces of fabric to the lower branches and made a wish. I have also found lots of coins in the clearing by these trees and this is because people use really low denomination kopec coins to make a wish. It was minus 6 deg C at our forest stop, but bright and beautiful.

We continued a distance and Nikki and Sergei drifted back to sleep, but I was transfixed by the scenery, which reminded me a little of pictures I have seen of Canada, because it was all hills smothered in fabulous green and gold foliage.

We crested the hill and I could see the great watery mass of Baikal shimmering in the distance with Bolshoe Goloustnoe spread along the shore.

Valery continued about two-thirds of the way along the village road, before pulling up at the brightly-coloured wooden house of our host, Galena.

She was a very cheerful lady and had kindly cooked us breakfast, because around 10am is the normal breakfast time in this part of Siberia. So we sat down to buckwheat porridge, which Sergei explained is a traditional Russian dish, plus home-made pastries and thick apple jam.

After breakfast, we were asked to choose our bedroom and they were all lovely, but we picked the smallest one next to the stove, in case it's really cold. A traditional Siberian wooden izba such as this one has a stove right in the middle of the house, with the bedrooms, lounge and kitchen around it. There is also a further outer hallway for taking off shoes and coats etc.

There is no bathroom in the house and traditionally there would be no running water, though there is an internal sink for washing your hands and brushing your teeth. The toilet is of the long-drop composting type and is right at the end of the garden. It doesn't smell at all and seems very efficient.

The garden also contains the banya (sauna) and the well, plus lots of flowers and herbs. Fishing nets hang on one side of a building and fresh omul fish from Lake Baikal are drying in a row in the sun on one of the outbuilding. They are the Siberian version of small salmon.

Having explored the house and garden, we unpacked a little before going for a walk around the village with Sergei. He takes us right to the shore of Lake Baikal and then to the old church on the lakeside. We climb the hill to a vantage point and sit down.

Here, we have the most amazing view over what is virtually the narrowest point of Lake Baikal – the far shore is approximately 40km away and its mountains are covered in snow.

After a while, we got up and walked through the woodland and Sergei showed us how they ate larch needles – I sampled them and found they taste a bit lemony at this stage of the autumn. Apparently they are sharper-flavoured in spring.

We got talking about our families and Sergei has two daughters aged 21 and 14, but his wife died of cancer three years ago, aged just 37. I could have wept, because as well as Jeremy, I have lost two other young friends to different forms of cancer, aged 23 and 42.

Hearing Sergei talk about the loss of his wife and the effect it had on him and his daughters reminds me of the Earl Mountbatten Hospice and just how lucky we are on the Isle of Wight to have somewhere that helps the families of terminally-ill people to prepare for what lies ahead.

We went across to look at the river, which seemed even colder to my fingers than Lake Baikal and Sergei told us of how he was born inside the Arctic Circle and rode horses when he was growing up. When he was 18, he was conscripted into the Russian Army and served at a camp in the Gobi Desert in Mongolia. Although he now lives in Irkutsk, he would love to return to the Gobi one day and visit his former base.

We walked back through the village to Galena's house in the early afternoon sun. On entering, we found she was just serving up lunch, including schee, which is a traditional soup eaten with dollops of mayonnaise, plus pasta and meatballs with sliced tomato and freshly-made coleslaw, followed by pastries, biscuit and sweets. Wow!

After lunch, Nikki decided to have a little nap (I think she's got my cold), while I took a walk down to the shore with the idea of having a paddle. I had my travel towel with me and while paddling, I started thinking that it wasn't too cold, so I stripped down to my knickers and went in.

I ducked down under the water right up to my neck, counted to eight or so and decided it was very cold really – must be minus something, so I got out, dried myself carefully and re-dressed, minus the wet knickers. Then I sat in the sunshine and texted Mum and Hugh.

The local dogs came over, plunged into the lake for a drink and then lay down in the sun beside me. I sat day-dreaming as I looked out over the vast shimmering lake, which is nicknamed The Pearl of Siberia.

Lake Baikal is one of the wonders of the natural world. Many people describe it as the most voluminous lake in the world by virtue of the fact it is the deepest lake on the planet and measures more than one mile in depth. Incredibly, it holds more than one-fifth of the world's fresh water and it has a surface area the size of Belgium.

It is some 636km long and is home to approximately 2,630 species of flora and fauna, around 75 per cent of which are not found anywhere else in the world, so it is an ecological gem, as well as a visual one.

In winter, the lake freezes over with ice more than a metre thick and cars can drive across it, while in summer, its crystalline depths are transparent to a depth of 40 metres and its shores are ringed with the brilliant colours of seasonal wildflowers.

I find myself thinking about Tracey's party, who have gone to the nearby village of Listvyanka, which is also on the shore of Lake Baikal and is known for its beautiful wooden izbas. Hope they are having a dip in the lake too!

Legend has it that those brave enough to take a dip in Baikal will add years to their life. If you put a hand or a foot into the water, you will gain an extra five years, whereas if you submerge your whole body – as I have done – you will add at least another 25 years of life. It is an interesting thought.

By 4pm, I decided to return home and I found a little shop on the way, so I bought some Baikal vodka to toast our colds later.

Back at the izba, Nikki and I got ready for our initiation into the banya, which is a Russian version of a sauna. It consisted of three rooms, a cool one, a medium one and a hot one. It was unusual in that you could wash your hair and body in the hot area, splash yourself down with cold water, lay out in the heat, splash down with cold water again and so on – a really lovely experience.

Afterwards, I returned to the izba to do a little bit of writing – the first today. Siberia is also proving to be an assault on my senses, but in another way. There is still brilliant blue sky, complete silence, a warm sun and startling foliage colours including green, gold and orange. But everywhere you tread you will also crush herbs growing underfoot, so it is fabulously fragrant too.

What with a day of just ambling around in the countryside, a dip in the mighty Baikal, a banya and a comfortable bed that isn't moving, I felt deeply relaxed tonight. You really can get away from it all here.

Galena had cooked a fabulous dinner including pelmeni (stuffed dumplings) and then we all had three toasts of Baikal vodka and followed the tradition of dipping the ring finger of the right hand into the vodka and laying a drop on the table for great Baikal, flicking a few drops into the air for the spirits and then placing a drop on our hearts for a wish.

After that, we got the DVD player going with a film about Lake Baikal and we were about 15 minutes into it when the fuse blew, plunging us into darkness. Galena went to the fusebox, I grabbed a torch and followed her and we soon had it sorted out.

Sergei decided he would like to go to bed and Galena lives in one of the outside buildings, so they bade us goodnight and Nikki and I finished the film on our own, before going to bed at about 10.30pm. I was asleep in minutes.

Beautiful Baikal

Saturday, October 4, 2008

I SLEPT right through until 9am! I don't think I have done that in years – I must be so chilled-out here.

Sergei has a theory that the word for Siberia also comes from the Latin word that spawned the English term 'severe', which could be right. It doesn't seem particularly severe in Siberia this morning. There is a frost, but it is another day of blue sky and golden sun.

We enjoyed a breakfast of eggs and sausage, plus pastries with apple jam and then at 11am-ish we set off along the lakeside path with Sergei with the aim of having a good walk across to the forestry camp for lunch.

Sergei thought it was about 6km each way, while Galena said it was nearer 8km each way, but it was a beautiful morning and we were soon striding out along the track. Lake Baikal shone the most brilliant blue and the forest was extraordinary shades of green, gold and deep red. We were soon joined by the Siberian husky who sat with me on the lakeside yesterday, though he disappeared after a while.

Once we left the village, the path branched off of the road and became narrower and started to wind through the trees. It plunged up and down quite a lot and then came out on the cliff face, where it remained parallel for some time. I luckily don't suffer from vertigo.

It was a long walk in the sunshine and we came across regular campsites where people had made fires. Sergei amused me by telling us that the Cossacks used to ride their horses along this narrow trail on patrols to catch people who tried to cross from the other side of the lake.

I thought the trail was far too narrow and close to the cliff edge for a horse, but I was proved wrong when I saw horse-dung on it – people obviously still ride along this trail today, which I find amazing.

We eventually arrived at the forestry camp at about 1.30pm and Sergei told us we could relax on the shoreline for a moment while he went up to the buildings and checked that our hosts had lunch ready.

The next thing I knew, Nikki was threatening a Baikal splash! So we stripped naked and both plunged in amidst lots of giggling. I thought it was only marginally warmer than yesterday and stayed under for about ten seconds while Nikki took my picture. I tried to return the gesture, but the camera kept flashing its battery light at me, so I snapped her coming out of the water.

Sergei came halfway down the track during our Baikal splash, realised what was happening, averted his eyes and called to us that lunch was ready when we were. We went laughing back to the shore, dried ourselves on my fleece jacket, dressed and went up to the forestry camp, where we met Alexi and his wife Irina, who had very kindly cooked lunch for us.

What a lunch it was! To start, we had fish soup containing the local Baikal fish omul, which was a little bit like salmon and absolutely delicious. This was followed by chicken and pasta, then bliny-style pancakes with rhubarb jam and tea.

One of the sons came in and offered us vodka, so we each had two shots with some peppered sausage. The young man told us of how he hoped to go to China and how he had recently 'killed' his car – he's only 22! Sergei said he was envious – he is in his 40s and has yet to own a car.

After lunch, we said goodbye to the foresters and they told us they had measured the water temperature today and it was only 9 deg C! They also told us we could walk along the beach for some distance to avoid some of the steeper sections of track and it was quite good fun – though I slipped off a rock at one point and put my toes in the water!

Later we followed the trail back up into the woodland and there were loads of families cooking in the open air and generally enjoying themselves – Sergei explained that Russian people love to come to Baikal for day trips and short breaks.

We were soon rejoined by our husky friend who led us part of the way back into town before disappearing off again – I think he may live in the house with the large Lenin head in the garden, which was rescued from a nearby town.

As we approached the church, we saw a herd of Buryat horses coming and I took a few pictures. Buryat horses are bigger than Mongolian ones, but are still tough and wild – though one grey horse stopped to sniff my fingers.

Sergei remembered that we were in time for the church service, so we popped into the church on the lakeside to take a look at the evening mass. I was aware that I should cover my forearms, so I put my jacket on, but I suddenly realised I didn't have a headscarf to cover my hair. Fortunately the lady who was singing spotted us and handed us some headscarves to wear – they must be used to visitors.

The church was Russian Orthodox and absolutely beautiful

inside with many paintings of Jesus and the Virgin Mary. The evening mass involved lots of singing and the priest came in and out from behind the screen singing different short phrases, while the lady sang long sentences in the most beautiful voice.

There wasn't a terribly big congregation and we didn't stay for too long, but it gave us an insight into the Russian Orthodox church and for anyone who is visiting Russia, it is well worth going into a service to hear them sing.

Afterwards, we stopped off at the village shop to get more vodka for our colds and then went back to Galena's, where we enjoyed another stint in the banya before dinner.

Galena had cooked us chicken with mashed potato, followed by a lovely cake and we toasted each other with vodka again and fired up the DVD to see the second video about Lake Baikal – this time it is all about the different unusual Baikal animals, including the nerpa, which is a type of freshwater seal; brown bears; omul; Siberian marmots; ground squirrels and much more.

As we were walking earlier today, I also noticed Siberia has lots of flowers – not only is there the Siberian edelweiss, but there are also dianthus growing wild, plus striking blue aquilegia-like flowers and numerous Michelmas daisy types.

After watching the video, we wished Sergei and Galena goodnight and we all went off to bed for another night of blissful sleep.

Sunday, October 5, 2008

I WOKE at about 7.15am – back to a more normal time for me then! It was cold, but pleasant outside, another sunny day. I decided to walk down to the great lake and watch the sun rising.

I put my hand in the lake and it was fairly cold. I did some photos of the lake in the eerie morning light and watched people herding their animals out from their backyards into the grassland around the village. I spotted a few hay-stacks around, where local people had forked loose hay into big piles to feed their livestock later in the year.

I saw more Buryat horses and did some photos, but my batteries were soon out of juice again, so I wandered back to Galena's house, changed my batteries and sat down to do some more writing.

Breakfast was at 10am and Galena had made us a very tasty omelette, together with a plateful of spicy sausage, tomato, bread and olives, plus a swiss roll.

Nikki is having a bit of trouble with her back this morning – she has had some problems during the trip and we are both hoping it doesn't get any worse.

We were just finishing breakfast when our driver Valery arrived with Sergei and Galena's next charge, Christie, so we all budged-up and they sat down to breakfast.

Christie was a larger-than-life character. This 32-year-old Australian admitted instantly that she was hung-over and had drunk far too much Chingghis Khan vodka on her way from Mongolia overnight.

She said she was a lawyer from Sydney and was spending a long time travelling to consider what to do next, because she wasn't really happy with her job. She kept us entertained for half-an-hour with her tales of drinking koumiss and really not liking it.

Christie then decided she would like a rest, so she went off to bed for a couple of hours. We weren't leaving until

1pm, so Sergei decided he would come for one final walk with us and I fancied one last dip in the lake (my third!), so I took my trek towel out and we all walked down to the lakeside and Nikki and Sergei continued walking while I stripped off and plunged in.

I was just swimming a couple of lengths because it was quite pleasant this morning, when I realised that I had attracted quite an audience! Not only were the two adorable Siberian husky pups which had followed me down onto the shore looking on, but a family of about five or six Russians were gathered there too.

I came out of the water slightly tentatively as I was completely naked, and the red-headed Russian lady spoke – I imagine she asked what the water was like, so I tried to indicate 'middling.' She promptly stripped off and went in, shrieked, splashed about a bit and came out laughing.

Two other young ladies joined us, together with a middle-aged lady, and they all rolled up their trousers and paddled in – that was it, I had started a Baikal splash party! What fun!

Having stretched out on the grassy bank for a few minutes, I dried off and got dressed, still fending off the excitable puppies – one of which had got hold of the mesh stuff-net that my trek towel goes in and was having a great game with it.

I left the party on the lakeside and walked back towards Nikki and we went along the shore for some distance before circling back through the village to Galena's house.

One of the things that has been puzzling Nikki and I during our stay in Bolshoe Goloustnoe is that all the houses have a little plaque on them – some have what looks like an ice-cream cone, some have rakes and some have shovels.

We asked Sergei and he explained that Galena had said they depicted each family's role in the event of a fire, because the village is many miles from the nearest fire station. Those with rakes would pull off burning roof materials, those with shovels would bury fires with dirt and those with ice-cream cones (which are actually water buckets) would douse the flames with Baikal water.

When we got back, Galena made us a cup of tea and offered us more slices of cake before we left. Valery had brought our passports back and our rail tickets, and although he does not speak much English, he was able to explain the carriage and berth numbers. Sergei asked him if he would take us somewhere to change money and then on to the rail station.

We made our farewells to Sergei and Galena and got into the car with Valery, who started the long drive back to Irkutsk – much of which is along unmade roads. He had some kind of slow puncture on one of the rear tyres along the way and stopped to pump it up.

Irkutsk is widely described as Siberia's eastern capital and lies at the crossroads of old tea, silk and fur trade routes between western Russia and China. The gateway to Lake Baikal, Irkutsk is often called the Paris of Siberia. It was also the city to which the Decembrists were exiled in the 1820s.

Valery gave us a bit of a tour of the city and showed us different churches and parks, before taking us to Hotel Irkutsk to change money, then on to the railway station in time to enjoy a cup of tea and a cake at the cafe. Then he escorted us to the Trans-Siberian, so we couldn't possibly catch the wrong train by mistake. What a star!

Once on the train, we discovered we were sharing a compartment with two large Russian guys. They didn't speak a word of English and I speak only three words of Russian, but it was clear they had lots of friends in nearby compartments.

Once we were on the move, one of their younger friends came into our compartment and picked up my phrasebook. He indicated 'food' and 'follow' to me and I thought he meant he was going to show me where the dining car was. So I followed him down the carriage and he led me into a nearby compartment where he and his friends had laid out a huge Siberian feast.

It turned out he was sharing a compartment with Tracey and Amanda and soon up to a dozen of us were packed in there – including Pat and Rachel – and lots of frantic translation and laughter transpired as it became clear the Russians wanted us to join in with their feast.

Over copious amounts of vodka; Siberian whisky; fresh fish from the Angara River which flows out of Baikal; chicken; pizza; potato bread; sausage and vegetables, we learned that this group of friends like to make people feel welcome in Siberia and they told us that Siberian people are very warm and friendly.

We learned that they all work together on a hydroelectric dam in Irkutsk, but they were going to Yeketerinburg (two days away on the train) for a holiday. As we all chatted, we also learned more about Rachel's scary story.

Our paths should not have crossed with Rachel and Pat again after Mongolia because they left on a train a day ahead of us. But Rachel and a Polish girl, who appeared to speak fluent Russian, got off the train at Ulan-Ude thinking they had 50 minutes at the station, so they went to a cafe.

Unfortunately when they returned to the platform, they found the train had left without them! But three teenage girls approached them and said not to worry, because there was a bus and they would take them to it.

So Rachel and the Polish girl got into the teenagers' car in good faith, but instead of being taken to a bus station, they were driven into a seedy area of town and beaten up by the three girls, who took their bags – including their passports and cameras – and ran off.

Rachel and her friend managed to find a guard, who took them to a police station, where they had to spend the night and fill in a million forms with the help of an interpreter. Luckily, Rachel's luggage was still on the train with Pat, who had insisted on keeping hold of it, even when the train staff had wanted to throw it off at the next station – unattended luggage is a possible terrorist threat.

Eventually Rachel, Pat and the luggage were all reunited and put back on our train, though Rachel still has no passport or camera, just document copies and a covering letter from the police.

When our Russian friends saw the bruises on Rachel's mouth and the scratches on her back, they were most unhappy that a visitor should be treated this way in their country.

They are a really nice bunch – there's Sergei and Sasha, who are in our compartment; then the younger Sasha who reads English and German; Anatoly, who's the group clown and is very funny; Alexander, who is quite quiet and Vladimir, who is a real gentleman.

During this highly social evening I must have had six or eight vodkas and whiskies before returning to my compartment and going to bed.

Train capers

Monday, October 6, 2008

I AM already suffering from train-time syndrome! This train runs on Moscow time, which means Irkutsk is +5 hours and then we work our way back. But the train crosses several time zones in a few short days, which should make for a very interesting experience.

For example, when I woke this morning, the train clock said it was 2.30am and it was pitch dark outside. But my watch said it was 7.30am, so it would already be light at Lake Baikal. But in truth, we have already crossed a time zone, or maybe even two, so in real terms it is an hour or so before dawn.

I think my Russian friends are similarly puzzled. They leapt out of bed at about 7.30am, went out and washed, then proceeded to return to the compartment and snooze until it was light. As I am sat here writing, it is almost 9am Irkutsk time, yet it is only half-light. Weird! I think the key is to eat, drink and sleep when you feel like it – then train life will be just fine.

A little bit later the guys went out for a while and Nikki and I brewed up some tea and broke open the cereal bars. We were just having some breakfast when Sergei and Sasha came back in with Anatoly, so we offered them all some cereal bars.

They declined and Anatoly indicated he had a hang-over, so we offered him and the others some vodka as hair-of-the-dog and they all accepted. Sergei gave us a bar of dark chocolate, which was really nice of him, while Anatoly indicated that we could go and eat with them anytime.

We stopped at Krasnoyarsk for a short time and I whizzed out onto the platform to buy a big bottle of Russian lemonade. Once the train moved off, I rejoined our Siberian friends for elevenses and we feasted on the remains of yesterday's picnic spread and before I knew it, I had consumed six vodkas – before midday too! I can't hold my pen straight now!

I note our friends do nothing but eat, sleep and drink and you know what they say – when in Russia, do as the Russians do!

When I returned to our compartment, I found Sergei and Sasha were both snoring their heads off, so I had a cup of tea and decided to have a little nap myself. Next thing I know, it's 2.45pm and Sergei and Sasha are up and about. Sasha (who is a great bear of a man) shambles out and Alexander comes in with beer for Sergei, who offers me a glass too. It seems they are happy to share everything!

They think it is funny that I am not writing and I try to indicate that I am not used to drinking vodka for breakfast in the morning. Sergei tops my glass with beer anyway and they gesture I should go back to sleep, so they leave me in peace.

The Siberian taiga (a forest of pine, larch and silver birch) is flying by and covers a large part of this extraordinary country. Apparently we are not too far from Novosibirsk, which is Siberia's largest city – although I suspect it might still be an hour or two away.

Just before 4pm, we stopped at Mariinsky and I dived out

onto the platform to find the enterprising babushkas selling a huge range of tasty treats, including blinys, freshly-cooked crayfish and dumplings. I bought some bliny and crayfish and took them back to Nikki, so we had a little feast in our compartment.

The bliny were filled with cottage cheese and were delicious, while the crayfish made a refreshing change, but as Nikki and I couldn't imagine any sea for thousands of miles, we concluded they must be freshwater crayfish from a nearby river.

Afterwards I was trying to write when Sasha came in and started being a bit amorous, so I got out Hugh's digital photo-frame and showed him pictures of my fiance and kept saying the word 'mooze' for married and pointing to my ring. Sasha seemed to get the drift of this, although he kept trying to kiss my hand and shoulder.

I decided to pop out and make a cup of tea and when I came back, Sasha had fallen asleep on my bed, so I went along the carriage a bit and popped in to see Rachel and we had a really good chat. She is still a bit shaken up by what happened to her, but seems to be coping well and now she just hopes she can get out of the country without her passport.

One by one, Pat came in, then Nikki arrived and said: "Have you seen the guys in our compartment?" So I take a peek and find Sasha is sprawled out on every available inch of my bed, while Sergei is asleep in his bunk with one leg hanging out. Both were snoring loudly, so I left them to it and wandered down to the dining car to join Nikki for a drink and some crisps.

Amanda joins us for a while – she has been hiding with some of the other Sundowners group members in first class. So together we all return to our carriage and discover Sasha is back in his own bed, as is Sergei, and they are both fast asleep. Anatoly was snoring like mad in his own bed in Tracey's compartment and she was happily using her laptop. Rachel and Pat had been joined by their two Russian compartment-sharers, Alexander and Vladimir, who were much quieter company.

Nikki and I went back to make our own beds and discovered our Russian compartment friends had a) been drinking our vodka – though I don't mind because we have been eating their food, but b) have spilt liquid all over my books, including this diary! Aarrgghh! So I mop up the mess and as they are pretty quiet in their bunks, I pick up my pen and start to write again.

Life with our Siberian friends is pretty funny – on the whole they want to share everything with us and they seem very cheerful. I just hope they aren't having serious romantic thoughts about us – I would hate to give anyone the wrong idea!

During the evening both Anatoly and Sergei poked and prodded Sasha in an attempt to wake him, but they couldn't. I prayed he was alright.

We stopped at about 9.45pm at Novosibirsk and got out for about 20 minutes. Nikki is in quite a lot of pain with her back and is in danger of seizing up, but walking around seems to loosen it.

We see people selling walking dog toys on the platform, which is rather amusing as they all seem to have boxes of the same toys. Nikki gets more bottled water, though I don't worry because I have got a big bottle of flavoured soft drink which our Russian friends don't seem to like, so it doesn't go missing suddenly!

After our platform venture, we get back on the train, I put my watch back another hour for the crossing of the time zone and we go to bed.

Tuesday, October 7, 2008

OUR Russian friends have been up and about a bit in the night, which is good because I had begun to fear that Sasha had died in the bunk above me!

I woke before dawn – I have given up trying to work out what time it is! I went and had a wash and dampened down and combed my hair back, as it looked like Fright Night. Then I came back to the compartment and laid down a while and waited for it to become light.

Nikki is clearly in a lot of pain with sciatica and cannot sit down or move around easily. We have indicated this to our Russian friends, who have unearthed a muscle rub for us to try, which might help. I have also given Nikki all my Anadin Extra, as she has nearly run out.

This morning we have managed to have some breakfast and have been making some plans. If Nikki isn't better later, I am going to ring ahead to The Russia Experience's Moscow office and see if they can find a chiropractor in the city.

Our Russian friends tell me the phrase I need for bad back is 'plukhoy speenah' and I write this down for use later. Rachel has also just volunteered to give Nikki a massage, which might help too.

One of the things I have been amazed about on this trip is how many young women there are out there travelling on their own whilst making up their minds what to do next. Look at Christie thinking about giving up being a lawyer. Or Rachel, who is coming back from performing theatre in

Korea and is looking for what to do next. Or Amanda, who has been teaching at summer camps and will grab the first job she sees when she gets home and then think about what she wants to do next. It is extraordinary how many brave young women there are out there seizing the opportunity to take control of their own lives and forge their own destiny.

And I? Will I join their brave new world? Or will I fall back into my job, which I have done for ten years and can do standing on my head. My nine-to-five job, which often seems tedious, but it pays my bills. Is the grass really greener? I wish I knew how one could tell.

Nikki comes back from her massage moving slightly better and we get out at Tyumen for a walk along the platform – alas there are no babushkas selling food here. According to Bryn Thomas in his Trans-Siberian Handbook, Tyumen is the only city in Asia to have hosted a European cup (football, I presume?) and is the oil capital of Western Siberia.

We get back on the train and have chicken and vegetable cup-a-soups, together with the remainder of the Chinese crackers. We have only a few cereal bars, the banana chips and some cup-a-soups left now, so we should manage to finish most of our supplies before we reach Moscow tomorrow afternoon.

I start writing again and as I turn the page, I realised I have done it – I have written 100 A5 pages during my trip and have succeeded in my challenge! I continue writing my diary with a big smile on my face.

I have to confess that I also love sitting and watching out of the train window for hours. We have only managed to travel a little bit of Russia during this trip, but what is clear is that it is an absolutely huge country – indeed I read somewhere that the UK would fit into Russia 69 times! Our journey has taken us past scores of towns and villages too, so there has been plenty to see.

Nikki is still very uncomfortable, so I try to ring Marlis Travel – our travel partners in Russia – to ask if they can find a chiropractor for Nikki, but I can't get through on either number. So instead I telephone the Hotel Irbis in Moscow and try to explain to them what I need. This turns out to be quite a palaver.

First of all, the girl on the telephone line doesn't understand which hotel I want.

"Which hotel?" she says.

"Hotel Irbis in Moscow", I reply.

"I am sorry, you must tell me which hotel," she continues.

"Hotel Irbis".

"I am sorry, if I don't know which hotel you are staying in, I can't help you".

"Hotel Irbis in Moscow". How much clearer can I be? Then I start to wonder is it pronounced Urbis or Earbis? I try both.

"Ahh yes, in Moscow. Which room are you in?"

I explain I am not currently staying at the hotel, but will be arriving tomorrow. She cannot get her head around this idea.

"If you are not staying at the hotel, I cannot see how we can help you."

"I will be arriving at the hotel tomorrow. I need a chiropractor".

The word chiropractor obviously does not exist in the Russian language. I try 'chiropractik' and do the 'plukhoy speenah' bit and I get passed round to several people, before being put in contact with the hotel's concierge. He understands me a bit better and I am beginning to explain myself quite well, but suddenly the line starts to break up and the next moment the signal cuts out completely and the line goes dead. Blast!

Nikki has been listening to my bizarre and rather lengthy telephone conversation and together we decide it may be best to wait until we get to Moscow and ask our English guide there.

Nikki wanted a lie down in the afternoon, but Sergei and Sasha had got all their luggage down in preparation for disembarking and they were asleep on their beds, so there was very little room to do anything. I shoved their bags off my bed so Nikki could lie down, then I took myself off to the dining car to watch the world go by over lemon tea and a packet of dried squid (bit salty and rather different to crisps).

Pat came in and joined me and we chatted for a while and when I returned to my carriage, I found Sasha had gone walkabout, so there was more room. Nikki had managed to have a bit of a rest and was thinking of going for a wander along the carriages, so I sat down on my bed and the next thing I knew, I was asleep! Train life is just SO taxing!

I slept for about an hour and woke up shortly before we pulled into Yeketerinburg. Many people like to spend a few days exploring Yeketerinburg because not only is it the gateway to the Ural Mountains which separate Europe and Asia, but it is Boris Yeltsin's hometown and widely-regarded as one of Russia's more colourful cities. It is also synonymous with the murders of the Romanov family during the Russian Revolution and they were transported to the town on the Trans-Siberian Railway.

Rachel and Pat are going to spend a few days exploring

Yeketerinburg while we go non-stop to Moscow, so we really shouldn't bump into each other again this time. We swap contact details.

Our Siberian friends are also getting off at Yeketerinburg – Anatoly gives me a big hug and a kiss on the cheek and I wave goodbye to Sergei, Sasha and the others, which is a bit sad really as they have been rather good fun and very generous with their food and vodka. Anatoly even admitted that he grew up in Bolshoe Goloustnoe and he knows Galena.

There was not much food being sold on the platform at Yeketerinburg, but I did manage to net a nice bag of oranges for later and when we got back on the train, we discovered we didn't have any new compartment-sharers, so it was absolutely undisturbed peace and quiet for a while.

A little bit later we ventured down to the dining car and had some dinner, washed down with some beer. While we were eating, we passed the unremarkable obelisk that pinpoints the Asia/Europe border, so we are now officially in Europe.

After dinner, we went back to our compartment and made our beds. No-one else has turned up to inhabit our upper bunks, though it is possible that someone might get on at Perm.

Perm is a popular place to stop off because it is particularly associated with Doctor Zhivago, the Nobel-Prize winning work, which was based on a Soviet-era banned novel by Boris Pasternak. It was set in Perm, where Boris Pasternak lived for some time and most of the book's locations are real places.

Nikki and I got off the train at Perm for a ten minute stroll along the platform. There were plenty of food kiosks, but nothing we particularly fancied. There was no-one in our compartment when we got back on the train, so we concluded that we have no new room-mates – though it is possible someone might get on at the next stop, which is at around midnight. I doubt we will make it to Moscow without being joined by someone!

On leaving Perm, I put my watch two hours forward to account for the forthcoming time zone and went to bed.

Wednesday, October 8, 2008

WE effectively went to bed at 8pm last night and gained two hours because of the time zone, so I have had nearly 12 hours sleep! Nikki has been up a while and is moving around a bit better this morning and we have a breakfast feast of oranges, cereal bars and banana chips. We are revelling in the fact we have still got the compartment to ourselves!

Winston Churchill described Russia as: "a riddle wrapped in a mystery inside an enigma", and it is a deeply fascinating country. It was ruled by Tsars for centuries, but repeated devastating defeats of the Russian Army during the First World War led to widespread rioting in the major cities of the Russian Empire and the overthrow in 1917 of the 300-year-old Romanov Dynasty by the Bolsheviks.

The Communists, under Lenin, seized power soon afterwards and formed the Union of Soviet Socialist Republics (USSR). The brutal rule of Stalin (1928-53) strengthened Russian dominance of the Soviet Union at the cost of tens of millions of lives. The Soviet economy and society flourished and then stagnated in the following decades until General Secretary Mikhail Gorbachov (1985-91) introduced glasnost (openness) and perestroika (restructuring) in an attempt to modernise communism.

But his initiatives inadvertently released forces that, by December 1991, had splintered the USSR into 15 independent republics. Since then, Russia has been building a democratic system and market economy to replace the strict social, political and economic controls of the communist era.

Today, Russia is a federation, with executive, legislative and judicial branches of government. President Vladimir Putin has served the country from 1999 until earlier this year (2008), when Dmitri Medvedev took over.

Russian life does still seem quite structured, but today's Russians are friendly, polite and helpful and are clearly much freer than just a few decades ago. Travel through Russia is also much easier – though English visitors must have a visa and clear itinerary and must have been invited to the country by someone in Russia – the elusive Marlis Travel in our case.

As the rural landscape slips by outside, I find myself thinking about this iconic railway. Although designed to bring great progress to Russia, it is hard to see how the many little villages along the track have been affected – much of the land is forested, while some is farmed in small plots around the villages and every dacha, or house, seems to have its own vegetable garden and perhaps a few chickens, a cow or a goat or two. People seem self-sufficient and most are toiling away and hardly even look up as the Trans-Siberian train goes by.

It's a grey day in Russia today with clouds and dull light more reminiscent of autumn in England – it reminds me that we are inching closer to home, but it is a bit of a shock after the brilliant blue skies of Siberia and Mongolia. One other thing that strikes me is just how endless Russia is – we have only seen a tiny ribbon of land rising from the border crossing at Naushki to Moscow, yet it has taken many days to cover.

I have discovered the Russians also have some smart inventions of their own – particularly at their railway crossings. They have barriers just like we do, but to prevent anyone just driving through, they also have metal plates which lift up to form a highly-visible barricade-style ramp. Their houses also have much steeper roofs than ours – presumably to help the snow slide off easier.

For railway enthusiasts, the Trans-Siberian offers a feast of different types on engine. Although our trains have all been diesel or electric, we have seen working steam trains in Mongolia and throughout Russia old steam locomotives are often mounted on plinths by the railway. There was even a big display of old locos by the station in Ulaanbaatar.

A couple of hours into the day we stopped at Nihzny Novgorod (aka Gorky), which is Russia's fourth-largest city. We got off for a walk along the platform and back, but we didn't see babushkas selling anything other than ice-creams.

Once back on the train again, we realised there is just one more stop before we reach our final destination – Moscow. I have also noticed how the landscape is changing – the silver birches are disappearing and there are more pines. This area of Russia also has many rivers. Obviously there is the great Volga, which is to Russia what the Nile is to Egypt. But there are lots of other rivers too and we regularly cross massive bridges with rivers flowing gently underneath.

Even here, about 350 to 400km from Moscow, the houses are almost all made from wood and the roofs are nearly all corrugated iron, which leads me to believe there are very few brick and tile manufacturers here. The land continues to change – now there are more oaks and elms appearing and it is marshier.

Nikki said she read somewhere that the average life expectancy of a Russian woman was 74, but a Russian man was only 59. I am not surprised in a country where vodka is as cheap as bottled water!

We stopped at Vladimir, the capital of the Suzdal area, but there wasn't much happening on the platform, so we went out for a quick walk, then went to the dining car to see what was on offer for lunch. I found the Salad Vzmorje – a mix of crabsticks, cucumber, sweetcorn and mayonnaise – quite refreshing. We tried to watch part of a Russian film in the dining car, but couldn't make a lot of sense of it.

On returning to our compartment, we packed up and watched the countryside fly by as we neared Moscow in the late afternoon. I was quite surprised how green Moscow appeared as we approached the Russian capital. Unlike London, we were only about 20 minutes from Yaroslav station when the landscape started to turn quite urban.

Yaroslav itself proved to be quite big with many platforms and we were amazed to think we were only a few minutes late arriving, not bad for a journey of nearly 5,000 miles from Beijing!

We said goodbye to Tracey, Amanda and the Sundowners group and went down the platform to meet our driver – who also turns out to be a Sergej (spelt differently but sounds the same.) He only speaks a word or two of English, but he took us through the heavy traffic in his minibus to the Hotel Irbis, which is close to the botanic garden. He makes sure we are able to register, hands me a piece of paper with details of tomorrow's city tour and then bids us goodbye.

After a very welcome shower and clean-up, we started

thinking about dinner and decided against going in to town. Instead, we opted to eat in the hotel's restaurant, which proved to be relatively expensive, but the spaghetti carbonara (I know, not very Russian) was the best I had ever tasted and the brown bread rolls were particularly nice.

We took a wander around our latest hotel and found the health centre, which does have a Turkish bath, a small pool and a massage room. I tend not to be too interested in these things, but I think Nikki might take advantage of it.

We picked up a few magazines and leaflets about Moscow from reception and went back to our room to watch a bit of television and read before bed.

Made it to Moscow

JUST in case we are complete train-nuts, Hotel Irbis is situated right next to a train station and we can hear them from our room! I think it must be a metro station though, because they don't appear to run all night.

The alarm went off at 7.30am, although I was awake before that because the trains started at about 5.30am and Nikki was up too. So we spruced ourselves up and went down for a big buffet breakfast with sausage, bacon, omelette, fruits in syrup and lots of other tasty treats.

After breakfast, I finally get to a computer to do my emails (hurrah – haven't managed to get to one since we left Ulaanbaatar!). After half-an-hour on the computer, I went back to our room to pick up my rucksack and get ready for our city tour.

When I was growing up, Moscow was the capital of an 'evil empire' which kept James Bond extremely busy. With the Cold War long gone, today's Moscow is the bustling nerve centre of Russia's cut and thrust in the democratic world. Despite this, the city is full of architectural wonders from another age, including the legendary Red Square, whimsical St Basil's Cathedral and Lenin's Mausoleum, not to mention the awesome gold-domed Kremlin, Russia's bastion of power.

Now I am going to see them all. Our method of transport for today is not a car or minibus, striving to forge its way through this city's terrible traffic, but the incomparable Moscow Metro. This amazing gift from Stalin to the people boasts famous chandelier and mosaic bedecked ticket halls and platforms and is a fast and efficient way to get around this giant city.

At a few minutes past 10am, our guide Elena meets us and takes us down through the clothes market to the metro. Our nearest stop is Petrovsko-Razumovskaya on the grey line and it's the only double-barrelled name on the whole metro, so it is easy to find on the map. We discover that on the metro, you can buy multi-tickets and share them between you, so we get a card for ten journeys.

Seven stops down on the grey line is Borovitskaya, which is the stop nearest the Kremlin gate. The Kremlin isn't open on Thursdays, but Elena showed us where we can get tickets tomorrow and told us what times the armoury is open.

We go down through Alexander Gardens past Manege, the old riding school; and on past the Hero Cities memorials and the Tomb of the Unknown Soldier, which has guards on duty and burns an eternal flame of remembrance.

Then we pass the statue of the man on the horse, which faces up one of Moscow's main shopping streets and go through the decorative gateway and into the renowned Red Square. Here we go past the National History Museum, and walk by Lenin's Mausoleum to the iconic St Basil's Cathedral.

Even though it is not particularly bright this morning (it's 9 deg C and overcast), the cathedral looks every bit as stunning as the many colourful photos I have seen of it.

Moscow has a long history, having become the capital of

Russia in 1164 AD. The first rulers held the title of Grand Prince of Muscovy and the first person to be called Tsar (a derivative of Caesar) was Ivan the Terrible, who ruled from 1547 to 1584.

Though generally thought to be a beastly person, Ivan was not completely terrible, as it was he who commissioned St Basil's Cathedral, which is surely one of the most popular visitor attractions in Russia. However, legend has it that he put out the eyes of the architect who designed St Basil's after completion, so that he could never design another building to rival the cathedral's beauty.

After taking lots of photographs of St Basil's, we went into G.U.M, the massive department store nearby. This was an eye-opener in itself and has three floors of shops, cafes and restaurants, as well as the most beautiful architecture, a large water fountain and a stunning glass roof.

Elena took us to see some of the other historical buildings around the city, including the Hotel Metropole, where parliament operated for many years, the Chekhov Drama Theatre and the Bolshoi Ballet, which is sadly closed for renovation until 2009. She also told us an amazing tale of how approximately 30 properties were moved to make one of the shopping streets much wider – they were placed on rollers and some were even moved while the residents were fast asleep inside! I can't imagine it, but it's an amusing tale all the same.

During the morning, Elena also helped us secure tickets for tonight's performance of La Traviata and inadvertently led us to believe that the opera was sadly extremely difficult to afford for the average Muscovite. Elena even found a good chemist to help Nikki select more painkillers – though my friend is moving a lot better today.

Elena's tour left us well-informed and well-orientated and after she bade us farewell, we went back to G.U.M. for a drink and a slice of cake and I discovered kefir, a type of drinking yoghurt which was really nice.

After that, we made our way through the bottom of Red Square onto the riverbank and went past the golden-domed Cathedral of Christ the Saviour and on past the statue of Peter the Great towering over the water. We continued past Gorky Park - which Muscovites call Kultury Park - made famous by Martin Cruz Smith's novel, which began with the haunting image of three bodies in the snow. I have vivid memories of reading it as a teenager, but never dreamed I might see the real Gorky Park – albeit not covered in snow or bodies!

We continued on to the home of Leo Tolstoy – probably Russia's most famous writer and the creator of the epic War And Peace and Anna Karenina, amongst others. His home is now an interesting museum, though strangely it is not mentioned in many guidebooks and I only discovered it via one of the flyers I picked up at the hotel reception last night.

At Tolstoy's house, we learned a lot about the great man himself and his family – particularly his wife, Sophia, who loved to knit and embroider, as well as helping Tolstoy with his work; and his daughter Maria, who helped her father with drafts and proofs. Another daughter, Tatiana, was an accomplished painter, while his sons all played musical instruments.

In its time, the house played host to numerous writers, painters, musicians and composers and it was extremely atmospheric – indeed when I walked into the great man's study, I almost expected to see Tolstoy himself sitting there writing. The house also has a particularly beautiful garden and the golden trees were mesmerising in the late afternoon sunshine.

After Tolstoy's house, we passed the Pushkin Museum of Fine Arts on our way back into the centre of town, where we stopped for dinner at a local restaurant and I sampled bortsh, the traditional Russian beetroot soup, and herring in a coat of grated carrot, beetroot and mayonnaise which was particularly delicious – must try to make that!

We went up the road to the theatre for La Traviata, which was a contemporary performance without English subtitles, but we had a handy English plot explanation and it was an extremely good show. We really got into the swing of things with a glass of Russian champagne each during the second interval.

After the performance, we successfully found Chekhovskaya metro station and negotiated our way around the metro on our own. Once back at Hotel Irbis, we enjoyed a celebratory shot of vodka in the bar before bedtime.

*

Friday, October 10, 2008

IT IS our last day in Moscow. We packed, had breakfast, did our emails and checked out at about 10am, though we left our luggage at the hotel and will collect it later.

We hopped on the metro down to Borovitskaya station and we went for a quick wander in Manege Shopping Court (which has a massive fast food hall underneath it!) before going to the Kremlin. All the guide books recommend spending a few hours at the Kremlin, which is the ancient citadel of Moscow and is essentially a walled city within a city.

The present stone and brick walls date back to the 16th Century and replace the previous wooden ones, which were destroyed by fire. Inside the walls, there are many government buildings, which are closed to the public. But visitors may go into the ancient cathedrals, where the Tsars were christened, crowned and buried.

Another popular part of the Kremlin for visitors is the Armoury, where all the treasures of the Tsars, including Faberge eggs, jewels and coronation regalia are kept. Unfortunately there were no tickets left for the Armoury and we couldn't get hold of an audio guide either, but we were able to look in all the lovely cathedrals – my favourite was the Assumption Cathedral, which was completed in 1479 on the site of an earlier cathedral and is jam-packed with extraordinary frescos dating from the 15th to 17th Centuries.

One of the most famous exhibits in the Assumption Cathedral is the throne of Ivan the Terrible (aka the Monomachos Throne), which was made in 1551. The Assumption Cathedral was not only the main church, but also an important public building. All coronations from 1498 to 1896 were held there, metropolitans and patriarchs were instated and important state edicts were proclaimed. Interestingly, religious services were reinstated in the cathedral in 1990 and it is still in use today.

Another real eye-catcher is the Ivan the Great Bell-Tower, which was erected between 1505 and 1508. The bell-tower acquired extra tiers on the orders of Tsar Boris Godunov in 1600 and now stands at 81 metres tall. Today, the bell-tower and belfry contain 21 bells, the largest of which is the Assumption Bell, which weighs around 70 tonnes.

However, stood outside the bell-tower on the paving is

the massive Tsar Bell, which weighs more than 200 tonnes and stands at more than six metres high. This bell was cast in the Kremlin in 1735 by Ivan Motorin. It was in the final stages of decoration when the terrible fire of 1737 broke out. As the fire was being put out, the bell cooled down too quickly, cracks started to appear and a piece of 11.5 tonnes broke off.

This damage meant the bell could never be rung and was abandoned for some time, until 1836 when it was lifted out of the moulding-pit where it had been cast and put on display. When I stood next to the Tsar Bell for a photo, I discovered the broken fragment was taller than me!

Nikki and I would have liked to have visited the Diamond Fund, which is a collection of the most amazing jewellery, but unfortunately it was closed for several hours for technical reasons, so instead we left the Kremlin and went in search of Stazny Arbat, or old Arbat Street, which has been described as the Covent Garden of Moscow. It was a rather long, but charming street lined with restaurants and souvenir shops, with painters and booksellers on stalls throughout its length.

We browsed through the stalls and souvenir shops and I saw an artist with one etching I particularly liked, but on making further enquiries, I realised it was a little more than I could afford. I didn't want to haggle because I could see it was of real quality, so I decided to leave it. The man tried to point me in the direction of other cheaper works, but it was only that one that really caught my attention.

After old Arbat Street, we decided it was dinner time, so we returned to G.U.M, where I had more kefir and herring in a coat, followed by Stolnichy chicken and Russian milk cake. Russian food is both varied and tasty, I have decided.

We just had time to look inside St Basil's cathedral, which is just as beautiful as any of the Kremlin cathedrals inside and is well worth a look.

By now, I realised we were running out of time and really should get back to the Hotel Irbis to pick up our luggage – particularly as I wasn't sure of the train route we had to take to get to the airport, but I knew the overland rail journey took around 50 minutes.

So we whizzed back to the hotel, grabbed our luggage and jumped straight back on the metro, changed to the green line at Chekhovskaya and went to Pavetskaya, where I successfully located the overland line. We caught the 6.30pm train and were miraculously at Domodedevo airport shortly after 7pm – around two hours before our flight took off, so panic over. Nikki said it was well navigated!

Check-in and security were trouble-free, even though we had been told they could take hours. In Moscow, they have a barrel-shaped structure which you stand sideways inside and it x-rays your whole body – weird!

Next, we did all the usual airport things, like spending our last roubles on chocolate and vodka at the duty-free shop. Nikki is hoping she will not seize up on the flight, but she has been moving a lot better in the last two days and is fairly confident that she will be able to drive home tomorrow.

We boarded the plane in good time, the flight took off on time and landed at Heathrow Terminal 5 a few minutes ahead of schedule. Nikki and I even had a glass of wine to celebrate our amazing trip whilst in the air and I didn't fall over afterwards!

Once at Heathrow T5, we went to baggage reclaim and our bags were there this time (hurrah!). We went out of the terminal and found a Hotel Hoppa bus almost immediately, which took us round and round the airport in ever-decreasing circles, before dropping us off at practically the last hotel on the route, Hotel Ibis.

We checked in and decided to have a quick shower, because we were both pretty hot and sticky after our mad dash across Moscow to the airport. It had been a very long day and it was just before midnight when we finally got to bed.

Saturday, October 11, 2008

BACK in Blighty! Unfortunately the hotel is quite close to Heathrow's plane park, so I am woken early by the sound of planes (well at least it makes a change from trains!) I lazed in bed for a while and then Nikki and I got up, had a shower and went down to breakfast – which Nikki insisted on paying for. It was an eat-as-much-as-you-like buffet, so I chose enough to keep me going for the whole day, including the eggs and bacon, fruit and yoghurt.

Throughout breakfast, I could see the television and all that was on was the doom and gloom about the burgeoning world financial crisis, which is all very depressing and quite a culture shock after almost three weeks of no news programmes.

After breakfast, we check out. Nikki has decided she is okay to drive home, so she is going back to T5 to get her car, while I need a Hotel Hoppa to go to T2 for the Central Bus Station to catch my coach home. So we bid goodbye to each other outside the hotel and I hop on the bus.

I am actually feeling quite emotional at leaving Nikki because we really have had the journey of a lifetime. We promise to keep in touch and send each other the big trip photos and I will call her later today to make sure she has arrived home okay. Despite problems with her back, she really has been a star on this trip and we have had a lot of fun.

On reaching the Central Bus Station at Heathrow, I open my diary and realise I have hit 120 pages – and raised thousands of pounds for the Earl Mountbatten Hospice in the process. It is hard to believe that after a journey that has taken me overland across a third of the planet, I shall very soon be home again.

I am extremely proud of what I have achieved.

THE END.